Quantum Computing
Questions and Answers

Ed Trex, Ph.D.

Contents

3 Quantum Bits (Qubits) 67

6 Quantum Error Correction   **133**

Preface

As we stand on the precipice of the third decade of the 21st century, we find ourselves confronted by a scientific revolution that promises to reshape the landscape of computation as we know it—quantum computing. In the echelons of computational and theoretical physics, a quiet yet profound revolution has been taking place, setting the stage for a future that was once only the fodder of science fiction. The advent of quantum computing stands to transcend the boundaries of classical information processing, promising an unprecedented leap in computational power and problem-solving prowess. It is in this exciting, dynamic context that this book, "Quantum Computing: Questions and Answers," was conceived.

Quantum computing—once a marginal, almost esoteric field—is increasingly pervading mainstream scientific discourse. The promise of exponential speedup for certain tasks has captured the imaginations of researchers, technologists, and forward-thinkers worldwide. Yet, for all its potential, the complexity and counterintuitiveness of quantum phenomena present a formidable challenge for those eager to decipher its principles and applications.

"Quantum Computing: Questions and Answers" strives to meet this challenge head-on. This book is designed to guide the reader through the labyrinth of quantum concepts, unraveling complex ideas into digestible fragments of knowledge. Each chapter systematically explores the fundamental pillars of quantum computing, from the basics of quantum mechanics to the intricate architecture of quantum algorithms and hardware.

The unique format of this book allows for a versatile and engaging exploration of quantum computing. Each chapter is constructed around a series of carefully crafted questions, encouraging an active, inquiry-based approach to learning. These questions are designed to anticipate the curiosities and hurdles encountered when learning quantum computing, offering clear, concise, and insightful answers.

Despite being grounded in robust scientific and mathematical principles, "Quantum Computing: Questions and Answers" steers clear of unnecessary jargon and overly mathematical exposition. The book places a strong emphasis on conceptual understanding, aiming to illuminate the underlying principles that make quantum computing so fascinating and powerful.

As the title suggests, this book is not just a theoretical treatise; it also explores the practical realities of quantum computing. From discussions on current and future applications to the analysis of prevalent challenges and controversies, the book provides a realistic and balanced perspective on this rapidly evolving field. It also introduces readers to various quantum programming languages and platforms, providing an essential springboard into hands-on quantum computing exploration.

"Quantum Computing: Questions and Answers" is written for curious minds who wish to navigate the fascinating world of quantum computing. Whether you are a student, a computer scientist, a seasoned researcher, or an enthusiast with a basic understanding of classical computing and a spark of curiosity, this book is for you.

In the end, this book seeks to demystify quantum computing, making it accessible and engaging for readers from diverse backgrounds. I hope that as you delve into the questions and answers that follow, you will share the excitement and awe that quantum computing evokes. As we embark on this quantum journey together, let's imagine, question, and discover the future of computing—one quantum bit at a time.

Enjoy the journey.

Chapter 1

Introduction to Quantum Computing

In the first chapter of our journey, we present an overview of quantum computing. We dive into the essence of what sets it apart from classical computing, exploring the unique principles that grant it its enormous potential. From the fundamental particles known as quantum bits to the vast landscape of quantum information processing, this chapter sets the stage for your quantum exploration.

1.1 What types of problems are quantum computers uniquely suited to solve?

Quantum computers are uniquely suited to solve a certain category of problems that classical computers struggle with due to their limitations in computation and speed. These computational tasks fall into three main categories:

1. **Factorizing large numbers:** Shor's algorithm, proposed by Peter Shor in 1994, demonstrates that quantum computers can factor large numbers exponentially faster than classical computers. This has significant implications, especially for cryptography where the safety of many current systems is based on the difficulty of factoring large numbers (prime factorization problem).

2. **Simulating quantum mechanics:** Feynman's proposal for a quantum computer was originally motivated by the desire to simulate generic quantum mechanical systems. Quantum mechanics is a linear theory, however simulating it on a classical computer involves exponentially many terms in the equations, making it computationally expensive. Quantum computers, which themselves operate based on principles of quantum mechanics, are better suited for this task.

3. **Searching large databases:** Grover's algorithm, proposed by Lov Grover in 1996, can search an unsorted database quadratically faster than a classical computer. While not providing the same exponential speedup as Shor's algorithm, this still represents a significant advantage over classical computers for certain problems.

Notably, these are not the only types of problems quantum computers are well-suited for, but they are some of the most recognized examples. Some other areas where quantum computers may excel include quantum machine learning, quantum optimization, quantum metrology, and solving certain types of differential equations.

Nevertheless, within the field of quantum computing, a key concept is the notion of "quantum advantage" (previously "quantum supremacy"). This is the milestone at which quantum computers are able to solve problems faster than classical computers can. While certain quantum devices have claimed to achieve quantum advantage for specific contrived problems, the realization of quantum advantage for practical problems remains an active area of research.

1.2 How could quantum computers impact industries such as pharmaceuticals or logistics?

Quantum computing promises to provide unprecedented computational power and remodel many industries including pharmaceuticals and logistics, amongst others. Here's how quantum computing could have an impact on these industries:

1. **Pharmaceuticals**: A primary challenge in drug discovery is the ability to simulate and analyze molecular interactions at an atomic level. Conventional computing has limitations in terms of both computational speed and capabilities. Quantum computing offers promising solutions here. Through quantum molecular simulation, researchers can analyze every possible interaction between drug compounds and biological molecules, which could lead to improved drug design and faster time to market.

2. **Logistics**: In logistics, companies often need to solve complex optimization problems - for example, how to route deliveries in the most efficient way when there are multiple variables like traffic, weather, parcel priority etc. Quantum computing can solve these types of problems far more efficiently than classical computers, leading to significant improvements in efficiency and cost savings.

To dig deeper, let's consider an example in each of these industries.

Pharmaceuticals Example: With quantum computing, researchers could use the principle of superposition, which allows quantum bits (or qubits) to exist in multiple states at once, to simulate multiple molecular interactions at once. A quantum computer could predict the outcome of these simulations much more quickly, thereby significantly reducing the timeline for drug design and development.

Logistics Example: Quantum computing could be used to solve the "traveling salesperson" problem, a well-known example of an optimization problem in logistics. If a salesperson has to visit a number of different cities, what is the most fuel- and time-efficient route they should take? Quantum computers can solve these problems much faster than classical computers because they can use the power of quantum superposition and entanglement to store and process a large number of possible solutions at once.

Please note that quantum computing is a rapidly evolving field and much of its potential is still theoretical. However, research is ongoing and there are optimistic indications about its future applications.

A significant part of progress depends on the ability to increase the coherence time of qubits and to build fault-tolerant, large-scale quantum computers, which enables the practical implementation of complex quantum algorithms. In the meanwhile, it is important for different industries, including pharmaceuticals and logistics, to actively monitor developments in the field of quantum computing and be ready to adapt and incorporate the technology.

1.3   What limitations do classical computers have that quantum computers can potentially overcome?

Classical computers have several limitations that quantum computers potentially overcome. These limitations stem mainly from classical bit-based, sequential computational methods and restrictions in manipulating and storing large and complex sets of data. Quantum computers, with their quantum mechanical properties, allow us to surpass these obstacles.

Let's outline some key limitations of classical computers that quantum computers aim to tackle:

1.   **Limited processing speed and power**: Classical computers perform operations sequentially, which can be time-consuming for complex calculations. Whereas, quantum computers leverage quan-

tum bits (Qubits), which can be in a superposition of states. This enables them to perform multiple calculations simultaneously, potentially providing exponentially higher processing speed and power.

2. **Handling complex problems**: Classic algorithms increase polynomially (or worse) in time and resource consumption as problem size grows. However, Quantum computing shows promise in solving complex problems with significant computational demands (such as factorizing large numbers, searching within unsorted databases, simulating quantum systems, and optimizing complex systems) more efficiently than classical computers.

3. **Energy efficiency**: As classical computers continue to progress according to Moore's Law, reaching limits of miniaturization brings new challenges including significant energy consumption, heat dissipation issues, and limit of transistor size due to quantum tunnelling effect. The quantum computer's potential for using entanglement and superposition principles may provide a path to more energy-efficient computing.

It's worth mentioning, however, that quantum computers aren't silver bullets and not meant to replace classical computers. They're designed to solve certain types of problems more efficiently, providing critical and complementary support to classical computing.

Here's a simple comparison table that might help:

In conclusion, while quantum computing presents an exciting avenue to surpass limitations innate in classical computing, it is still under active research and development to fully realize its potential. Further breakthroughs in both theoretical algorithms and practical hardware are needed.

	Classical Computers	Quantum Computers
Bit	Bit either represents 0 or 1.	Qubit can represent 0, 1, or both due to superposition.
Operations	Operates sequentially.	Can perform many operations simultaneously.
Problem Complexity	Struggles with exponential scaling for complex problems.	Can potentially handle exponentially complex problems efficiently.
Energy Efficiency	Energy inefficiency due to heat and miniaturization issues.	Potentially more energy efficient through quantum mechanics principles.

Table 1.1: Comparison of Classical Computers and Quantum Computers

1.4 How is the concept of "quantum speedup" related to the need for quantum computing?

Quantum speedup is at the foundation of the need for quantum computing. Essentially, quantum speedup refers to the potential for quantum computers to solve some types of calculations significantly faster than their classical counterparts, thereby solving problems that would otherwise be practically impossible to compute due to the computations' sheer scale.

To better understand the concept of quantum speedup, we can look at the example of Shor's algorithm - a quantum algorithm for integer factorization. Classical algorithms for this problem require steps that grow exponentially with the size of the input, but Shor's algorithm only needs steps that grow polynomially with the input size. This is why a quantum computer using Shor's algorithm can factorize much larger integers in a reasonable time frame than any classical computer.

Theoretical time complexities of Shor's algorithm and best known classical algorithm can be simplified as follows:

- Classical: The best known classical algorithm is the General Number Field Sieve (GNFS) with time complexity approximately
$\exp\left(64\left(\frac{\ln N}{3}\right)^{1/3}(\ln\ln N)^{2/3}\right)$

- Quantum (Shor's algorithm): $O((\log N)^2(\log\log N)(\log\log\log N))$

where N is the number to be factorized. This clearly shows the quantum speedup.

Aside from computational speed, the concept of quantum speedup also applies to space, or the amount of memory required by a computer to solve a given problem. In certain instances, quantum computers can solve problems using exponentially less memory than the equivalent classical computers.

Hence, the quantum speedup — both in terms of computational time and memory space — justifies the need for quantum computing. They are desired for solving complex problems, especially in the areas of cryptography, optimization and simulation of quantum physics, where classical computers fall short due to their computational capacity according to Moore's law.

1.5 What is the current status of quantum computers in terms of their capabilities and limitations?

The field of quantum computing has seen exponential growth over the past few years due to advancements in technology and increased investment in research and development. Quantum computers are machines that use the principles of quantum mechanics to process information, providing a significant speedup over traditional computers for certain tasks.

Let us discuss the capabilities and limitations of quantum computers as of now.

Capabilities:

1. **Quantum Supremacy:** Quantum Supremacy or Quantum Advantage is the ability of quantum computers to solve problems that classical computers cannot. Google's quantum computer, a 53-qubit Sycamore processor, recently demonstrated this by solving a problem in 200 seconds that would take a state-of-the-art supercomputer approximately 10,000 years to solve.

2. **Solving complex problems:** Quantum computers can quickly conduct complex calculations, conduct simulations and solve optimization problems. They are especially beneficial for tasks like Factoring, Search problem, Simulation, Machine learning etc.

3. **Quantum Algorithms:** We already have various algorithms like Shor's Algorithm for factoring, Grover's Algorithm for searching, and many others which give exponential speedup compared to classical algorithms for the same task.

Limitations:

1. **Quantum decoherence and errors:** Even small errors during calculations can lead to large differences in outcomes. The current challenge is in maintaining qubits long enough in their delicate quantum states so that computations can be made.

2. **Scalability:** We need to isolate the system from all external influences to maintain coherence. The problem is that this makes it hard to interact with the information or to get the information out.

3. **Lack of efficient quantum algorithms:** For many practical problems, there does not yet exist a known method to solve them

faster on a quantum computer.

4. **Understanding and Training:** Quantum computers operate fundamentally differently from classical computers, requiring a shift in approach from developers and programmers.

To give some more insight, we can represent the number of qubits and the quantum volume which measures the effective number of qubits of IBM quantum computers in a simple table:

```
| Year | Number of Qubits | Quantum Volume |
|------|------------------|----------------|
| 2016 | 5                | Not Measured   |
| 2017 | 16               | 4              |
| 2018 | 20               | 4              |
| 2019 | 20               | 16             |
| 2020 | 27               | 32             |
| 2021 | 65               | 64             |
```

The field of quantum computing is still in its infancy with many technological and theoretical issues to overcome. However, the potential of quantum computing is enormous and its full realization would revolutionize many industries.

1.6 How does the quantum bit (qubit) fundamentally differ from the classical bit?

In classical computing, a bit is the fundamental unit of information that can exist in two states, represented as 0 or 1. However, Quantum Computing introduces a new fundamental unit of quantum information, the quantum bit or qubit.

The primary difference between qubits and classical bits is given by the fundamental principles of quantum mechanics: superposition and entanglement.

1. **Superposition**: Unlike a classical bit that can be either 0 or 1,

a qubit can be both 0 and 1 at the same time due to the principle of superposition. A qubit is represented as:

$$|\psi\rangle = \alpha|0\rangle + \beta|1\rangle$$

where $|\alpha|^2$ is the probability of the qubit being in state $|0\rangle$, and $|\beta|^2$ is the probability of the qubit in state $|1\rangle$. It's important to add that $|\alpha|^2 + |\beta|^2 = 1$, as the total probability must be equal to one.

2. **Entanglement**: Entanglement is another quantum feature which allows particles to become interconnected. The state of one particle becomes instantaneously correlated with the state of the other, no matter the distance between them. This property leads to exponentially more computational power. If two qubits are entangled, the state of one immediately influences the state of the other, regardless of the distance separating them.

These properties make qubits fundamentally different from classical bits. They allow quantum computers to process a large number of possibilities simultaneously, potentially solving certain complex problems much more efficiently than classical computers.

To elucidate this point further, let's consider an example: With three classical bits, we can represent any one of the eight different combinations at a time (000, 001, 010, 011, 100, 101, 110, or 111). However, with three qubits, due to the superposition principle, we can represent all eight combinations at the same time!

Keep in mind that when a quantum system is measured, it collapses to one of the basis states. So we generally can't access all those states at once despite their simultaneous existence due to the nature of quantum measurement.

This is only a brief introduction to a vast and complex field of study, and quantum computing research continues to evolve rapidly.

1.7 What do terms like "superposition" and "entanglement" mean in the context of quantum computing?

In quantum computing, "superposition" and "entanglement" are key concepts that define the fundamental behavioral difference between classical and quantum bits (qubits).

1. Superposition: In classical computing, the smallest unit of information is a bit that can take either the value 0 or 1, never both simultaneously. On the contrary, a quantum bit (qubit) can be in a state where it can be both 0 and 1 at the same time. This is known as superposition.

The quantum state of a qubit can be described as a linear superposition of its basis states:

$$|\psi\rangle = \alpha|0\rangle + \beta|1\rangle$$

Here, $|\psi\rangle$ denotes the quantum state. α and β are complex numbers, and $|0\rangle$ and $|1\rangle$ are the basis states, which are akin to the classical 0 and 1. The probabilities of the qubit being in $|0\rangle$ or $|1\rangle$ when measured are $|\alpha|^2$ and $|\beta|^2$, respectively, and $|\alpha|^2 + |\beta|^2 = 1$.

2. Entanglement: Entanglement is a counter-intuitive quantum phenomenon in which qubits become interconnected. When qubits are entangled, the state of one qubit becomes linked to the state of another, no matter the distance between them. It means that the state of one qubit can instantly affect the state of the other, even if they are light-years apart.

For two qubits, the entangled state could be represented in the form:

$$|\psi\rangle = \frac{1}{\sqrt{2}}\Big(|00\rangle + |11\rangle\Big)$$

In this state, if we measure the first qubit to be in the state $|0\rangle$, the second qubit will also be found in the state $|0\rangle$. Similarly, if the first qubit is measured to be in the state $|1\rangle$, the second qubit will also be found in the state $|1\rangle$, despite the separation distance.

These properties of superposition and entanglement are what gives quantum computers their increased computational power compared to classical computers.

1.8 How does a quantum computer process information differently than a classical computer?

Quantum computers process information fundamentally differently from classical computers by leveraging the principles of quantum mechanics. Quantum mechanics describes physics at the smallest scales, such as that of subatomic particles.

In traditional or classical computing, the fundamental unit of information is the bit, which can represent either a 0 or a 1.

However, in quantum computing, the fundamental unit of information is the qubit (short for "quantum bit"). Unlike a classical bit that can be in one of two states, a qubit can exist in a superposition of states. In other words, a qubit can be both 0 and 1 at the same time. Mathematically, the state of a qubit can be represented as

$$\alpha|0\rangle + \beta|1\rangle,$$

where α and β are complex numbers such that $|\alpha|^2 + |\beta|^2 = 1$, and $|0\rangle$ and $|1\rangle$ are the basis states.

This allows for a vast increase in computational power. If we have n qubits, they can represent 2^n different states simultaneously. This is in contrast to n classical bits, which can only represent one of the 2^n states.

Furthermore, quantum computation uses quantum gates to manipulate qubits in a reversible way. This is different from classical gates which are generally not reversible. Quantum gates are unitary operators and can perform complex operations on a superposition of input states. Because of the properties of quantum mechanics, the operation of quantum gates can also involve entanglement and interference, leading to the potential for much more complex computation.

To fully exploit these powerful characteristics of quantum computers, we need to design and implement quantum algorithms, which are fundamentally different from classical ones.

Of course, it's worth noting that the real potential of quantum computing, especially in regards to outperforming classical computers in practical tasks, is still a topic of ongoing research. Existing quantum computers are not yet able to outperform classical computers on most practical tasks due to limitations in size, error rates, and coherence times. However, the theoretical potential of quantum computing remains immense and is the subject of extensive research and development.

1.9 In what scenarios can a classical computer outperform a quantum computer?

There are several scenarios where classical computers can outperform quantum computers. Quantum Computing is undoubtedly powerful, but its power primarily lies within specific computational tasks. Here are some key scenarios where classical computers have the advantage:

1. **Classical Data Tasks**: For tasks involving classical data, like simple data input/output, writing and reading to disk, browsing the web, using spreadsheets and word processors, classical computers perform more efficiently than quantum computers.

2. **Error Correction**: Quantum computers have no inherent error correction, which makes them sensitive to environmental noise,

reducing their effectiveness. Classical computers, on the other hand, have mature error correction techniques.

3. **General-Purpose Computation**: Quantum computers excel at particular kinds of tasks (such as factoring large numbers or simulating quantum systems). However, for general tasks, a classical computer can be much faster and more reliable.

4. **Code Compilation and Debugging**: Quantum Computing involves complex algorithms, and often it requires high-level optimization to convert these into an efficient program to run on a quantum computer. Classical computers are more efficient and user-friendly when it comes to tasks related to compiling and debugging.

5. **Algorithm Complexity**: Some algorithms like binary search, merge sort, breadth-first search, among others, have a well-defined, efficient classical complexity. Converting these algorithms for quantum computation might not give significant speed-up or could be more complex.

Here's a simple comparison chart for reference:

Scenario	Classical Computer	Quantum Computer
Classical Data Tasks	Strong	Weak
Error Correction	Strong	Weak
General-Purpose Computation	Strong	Weak
Compilation and Debugging	Strong	Weak
Problem-specific Algorithms	Variable	Variable

Table 1.2: Comparison of Classical Computers and Quantum Computers on different scenarios

Remember, just as classical computing took decades to mature, quantum computing is still in its early stage and is likely to evolve to address many of these limitations over time.

1.10 Why can't quantum computers simply replace classical ones?

There are several key reasons why quantum computers can't simply replace classical ones, despite their superior computational power for certain tasks.

1. **Quantum computers are difficult to build and maintain**: Quantum computers require specific conditions to function, such as extremely low temperatures, to minimize thermal fluctuations and noise. This makes them far more delicate and difficult to build and maintain than classical computers, which operate reliably under a wide range of conditions.

2. **Not all tasks benefit from quantum computing:** Quantum computers excel at certain tasks, like factoring large primes, simulating quantum mechanics, or executing certain search algorithms more efficiently than classical computers. However, for many everyday computational tasks, classical computers are not just adequate, they're more efficient. This means there's currently no practical need to replace classical computers with quantum ones in many applications.

3. **Error correction and noise**: Quantum systems are highly sensitive to slight changes in their environments. Noise can introduce errors in quantum computations, and standard error correction methods used in classical computation do not efficiently translate to quantum computation.

4. **Coherence time**: Quantum bits (qubits) can only maintain their state for a brief period of time (known as the coherence time) before they start losing information due to environmental factors. In comparison, classical bits can store information indefinitely.

5. **Programming complexity:** Programming a quantum computer is very different from programming a classical one. Only a limited number of people currently possess these specialized skills.

6. **Reading the results correctly:** Measurements on a quantum system can be probabilistic, meaning you may need to run an algorithm several times to get a reliable result.

Here's a simple table that highlights some of the key differences:

Comparison	Quantum Computer	Classical Computer
Processing	Uses qubits (which can exist in multiple states at once - superposition)	Uses classical bits (which can be either 0 or 1)
Nature of Operation	Can perform many calculations concurrently through quantum parallelism	Sequential calculations
Environment	Requires extremely controlled conditions	Can work in general everyday conditions
Speed	Superior speed for certain tasks	Generally faster for everyday tasks
Interference	Highly sensitive to interference	Less sensitive to interference
Programming	Requires specific quantum algorithms	Uses numerous well-known classical algorithms

Table 1.3: Comparison of Quantum Computers and Classical Computers

In summary, while quantum computers hold immense potential for certain applications, the replacement of classical computers is neither practical not feasible in the near future. This is primarily due to the significant technical challenges involved in constructing and maintaining quantum computers, and because classical machines continue to work effectively for most computational tasks. As the field of quantum computing advances, we may find more effective solutions to these limiting factors, enabling more widespread use of quantum technology.

Chapter 2

Basics of Quantum Mechanics

This chapter takes us on a journey through the surreal landscape of quantum mechanics. From the formulation of quantum states to the principles of superposition and entanglement, and the fascinating concept of quantum teleportation, we seek to lay a robust groundwork for your quantum understanding.

2.1 What are the fundamental properties of a quantum state?

In quantum mechanics, the state of a quantum system is fully described by a vector in a mathematical space, known as Hilbert space. Two fundamental properties of a quantum state are superposition and entanglement.

1. **Superposition**: In classical physics, systems can be in one

state at any time; however, in quantum mechanics, things can be in several states at the same time. This is the principle of superposition. A quantum particle, such as a photon, can be in multiple states simultaneously. If we denote two states as |0> and |1>, the state of a qubit (quantum bit) can be written as:

$$\alpha|0> +\beta|1>$$

Here, α and β are probability amplitudes and can in general be complex numbers. The probability of the qubit being in state $|0>$ is given by $|\alpha|^2$ and in state $|1>$ by $|\beta|^2$. One key feature of qubits is that due to superposition, they may be in a state where the probabilities of measuring the state $|0>$ or $|1>$ are not 100% certain, but depend on the coefficients   and , and this permits the simultaneous processing of a vast number of states.

2. **Entanglement**: Entanglement is another unique feature of Quantum Mechanics. When particles are entangled, the state of one particle cannot be described independently of the state of the other particles. They form a single, entangled state, and a measurement on one part of the entangled system can affect the outcomes of measurements made on the rest, irrespective of the distance separating them. This is counter-intuitive to our everyday experience and is not found in classical systems.

A pair of entangled qubits can be in the state:

$$1/\sqrt{2} * (|00> +|11>)$$

In this state, if the first qubit is measured and found to be in state $|0>$, the second qubit is instantly known to also be in state $|0>$, no matter how far apart they are. Similarly, if the first qubit is found in state $|1>$, the second qubit will be in state $|1>$.

These two properties, superposition and entanglement together, are the key to quantum mechanics and quantum computers that take advantage of these properties to solve certain types of problem more efficiently than classical computers.

2.2 What does the term "state vector" mean in quantum mechanics?

In quantum mechanics, a "state vector" is a fundamental concept that describes the state of a quantum system. It is also known as a "wave function" in the context of the Schrödinger equation.

Formally, a state vector is a vector in a Hilbert space - a mathematical construct that allows us to quantify and study quantum states. The space is complex and infinite-dimensional; each point in this space corresponds to a possible state that a quantum system can be in. The state vector specifies the coefficients of a linear combination of basis vectors, which represents the system's state.

Let's denote our state vector by $|\psi\rangle$. In quantum mechanics, this abstract state vector provides the most complete description of a quantum system. From this state vector, we can calculate the probabilities of the outcomes of any measurement made on the system, as dictated by the Born Rule. If the ith possible state for a measurement has wave function $|\phi_i\rangle$, then the probability of arriving at this state when a measurement is taken is given by:

$$p(i) = |\langle\phi_i|\psi\rangle|^2$$

Where $\langle\phi_i|\psi\rangle$ is the inner product of the vectors $|\phi_i\rangle$ and $|\psi\rangle$, and $|\langle\phi_i|\psi\rangle|^2$ implies the modulus squared of the result.

Practically, each component of this state vector often represents the probability amplitude for the system to be found in a particular state. The absolute square of this probability amplitude gives the probability of finding the system in that state upon measurement.

Remember, the state vector will be a superposition of multiple vectors(each representing a specific state) in a general quantum state and will collapse to a particular state upon measurement. After measurement, the state vector will become the eigenvector associated with the measured eigenvalue.

Therefore, the state vector has immense importance in quantum mechanics as it allows us to predict the statistical outcomes of experiments.

2.3   How can we visualize the quantum state of a single qubit?

A qubit, or quantum bit, is the basic unit of quantum information. Unlike classical bits that can either be 0 or 1, a qubit can be in a superposition state, being in both 0 and 1 states simultaneously. This quantum state of a qubit can be visualized using a concept called Bloch sphere.

The state of a single qubit is expressed as:

$$|\psi\rangle = \alpha|0\rangle + \beta|1\rangle \qquad (2.1)$$

where $|0\rangle$ and $|1\rangle$ are basis states, α and β are complex numbers, and $|\alpha|^2 + |\beta|^2 = 1$, which ensures that the state is properly normalized (the total probability of finding the qubit in either state is 1).

These complex numbers α and β can be expressed in polar form as: $\alpha = r_1 e^{i\theta_1}$ and $\beta = r_2 e^{i\theta_2}$. Now we can leverage the Euler's formula and represent the quantum state of a qubit as:

$$|\psi\rangle = r_1 e^{i\theta_1}|0\rangle + r_2 e^{i\theta_2}|1\rangle \qquad (2.2)$$

This is where the Bloch sphere comes into play. It's a three-dimensional sphere where the state of a qubit is represented as a point on its surface. Here's why that works:

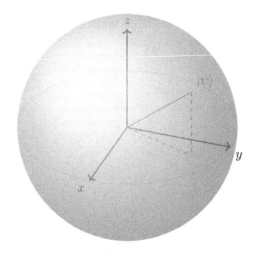

- The position around the horizontal axis of the sphere represents the relative phase between $|0\rangle$ and $|1\rangle$, which can be calculated from the difference in their individual phases θ_1 and θ_2 .

- The position above or below the horizontal plane represents the probabilities of the outcomes $|0\rangle$ or $|1\rangle$, which come from the magnitudes r_1 and r_2.

So, by mapping $|0\rangle$ to the top of the sphere (north pole), $|1\rangle$ to the bottom (south pole) and using the relative phase and probabilities, any qubit state can be represented as a point on the Bloch sphere.

As such, the Bloch sphere provides a useful means to visualize the state of a single qubit in quantum mechanics. However, it's important to note that its representation is largely abstract, and the motion of state vectors in this sphere doesn't correspond to a physical motion in real space.

2.4　How does the state of a quantum system change over time?

The state of a quantum system changes over time according to the Schrödinger Equation. The equation is given as:

$$\hat{H}|\psi(t)\rangle = i\hbar\frac{d}{dt}|\psi(t)\rangle$$

where:

- $|\psi(t)\rangle$ is the state of the quantum system at a time t,

- $\hat{H}$ is the Hamiltonian operator which represents the total energy of the system, and

- $\hbar$ is the reduced Planck's constant (also known as Dirac's constant).

The state $|\psi(t)\rangle$ is usually a complex-valued function with the property that its absolute square $|\psi(t)|^2$ gives the probability distribution for measurement outcomes. It is often called the wave function.

Using this equation, if the initial state $|\psi(0)\rangle$ is known, the future evolution of the quantum state can be described.

In quantum mechanics, we often use the time-independent Schrödinger equation to find the state $|\psi\rangle$, where the Hamiltonian $\hat{H}$ does not explicitly depend on time. The general solution to this equation is of the form:

$$|\psi(t)\rangle = e^{-iHt/\hbar}|\psi(0)\rangle$$

This is a unitary evolution, which implies that the total probability (the sum of the probabilities for all possible outcomes) is conserved over time.

2.5 Can a quantum state be cloned or copied exactly?

No, a quantum state cannot be cloned or copied exactly. This is known as the "no-cloning theorem" of quantum mechanics. The theorem was independently formulated by Wootters, Zurek, and Dieks in the early 1980s, and it is one of the key elements that differentiate quantum computing from classical computing.

The theorem states that an arbitrary quantum state cannot be precisely copied. More precisely, if we have a machine that makes copies, and we try to copy an arbitrary state $|\psi\rangle$, the combined state of the original and the copy will not be $|\psi\rangle\|\psi\rangle$.

To understand why this is significant, let's compare it to classical computing. In a classical computer, data is stored in bits. You can copy this data as many times as you want, and do so perfectly. But for quantum data, stored in quantum bits or qubits, this is not possible. This forms the basis of quantum cryptography and quantum communication protocols, such as quantum key distribution, which are secured by the laws of physics themselves.

To give a visual representation of the topic, consider the Bloch sphere representation of a qubit state:

$$|\psi\rangle = \cos(\theta/2)|0\rangle + e^{i\phi}\sin(\theta/2)|1\rangle$$

Here, $|0\rangle$ and $|1\rangle$ are the computational basis states, θ is the polar angle, and ϕ is the azimuthal angle. In the Bloch sphere representation, a state is defined by a point within the sphere—not just on the surface. The inability to clone or copy is visually represented by the inability to map all points within the Bloch sphere to another set of points within the sphere.

Here is the proof of the no-cloning theorem:

Mathematically, the no-cloning theorem is straightforward to prove. Assume that U is a unitary operator that clones a state $|\psi\rangle$:

$$U|\psi\rangle|e\rangle = |\psi\rangle|\psi\rangle$$

Here, $|e\rangle$ is a blank qubit state to which the information is copied.

Let's assume that $|\phi\rangle$ and $|\psi\rangle$ are two orthogonal states of a qubit.

According to the hypothesis of the clone, we should have:

$$U|\phi\rangle|e\rangle = |\phi\rangle|\phi\rangle \quad (1)$$

and

$$U|\psi\rangle|e\rangle = |\psi\rangle|\psi\rangle \quad (2)$$

Taking the scalar product of equation (1) with itself gives:

$$|\phi\rangle\langle\phi||\phi\rangle\langle\phi| = |\langle\phi|\phi\rangle|^2 = 1$$

Doing the same with equation (2) gives:

$$|\psi\rangle\langle\psi||\psi\rangle\langle\psi| = |\langle\psi|\psi\rangle|^2 = 1$$

However, if we take the scalar product of equation (1) with equation (2), we get:

$$\langle\phi|\psi\rangle\langle\phi|\psi\rangle = |\langle\phi|\psi\rangle|^2 = 0$$

This is due to the hypothesis of orthogonality ($\langle\phi|\psi\rangle = 0$). But if the machine perfectly cloned $|\psi\rangle$ and $|\phi\rangle$, we should have:

$$\langle\phi|\psi\rangle\langle\phi|\psi\rangle = \langle\phi|\phi\rangle\langle\psi|\psi\rangle = 1$$

We end up with a contradiction, stating that a perfect quantum cloning machine cannot exist.

In conclusion, the no-cloning theorem assures us that it is impossible to create an identical copy of an arbitrary unknown quantum state.

2.6   Can you provide an intuitive explanation of superposition in quantum mechanics?

Superposition is a key principle in quantum mechanics that holds the potential to explain the tremendous computing power of quantum computers. This principle allows quantum systems to exist in multiple states at once, i.e., a quantum system such as a quantum bit, or qubit, can be in a state 0 and 1 simultaneously. This is contrary to classical bits, which can be either in state 0 or 1 at any given time.

To understand quantum superposition intuitively, you might think of a coin spinning in the air. While it is spinning and not yet landed (not measured), it can be thought of as being both head and tail. It is in a superposition of both states. In this analogy, the instant of the coin landing is the measurement of our quantum system. And the nature of quantum mechanics, based on Born's rule, is such that when you measure this superposition system, you get one definite state, much like the coin that shows either head or tail when it lands.

A more precise description would entail complex coefficients. The state of a qubit can be written as:

$$|\Psi\rangle = \alpha\,|0\rangle + \beta\,|1\rangle$$

Where $|0\rangle$ and $|1\rangle$ are the base states, and α and β are complex numbers. The absolute squares of the coefficients, $|\alpha|^2$ and $|\beta|^2$, give the probabilities of the qubit collapsing to the corresponding states upon measurement.

In practice, a single qubit being in a superposition state does not provide much computational power. The real power lies in the ability of multiple qubits to exist in a superposition of states. For example, 2 qubits can exist in a superposition of 4 states, 3 qubits in a superposition of 8 states, and so on. Thus, the number of states a system of n qubits can exist in grows extraordinarily quickly as the number of n grows. This fundamental property makes quantum computers exponentially powerful than classical ones.

2.7　What's the relationship between superposition and quantum parallelism?

Quantum superposition and quantum parallelism are both integral concepts in quantum mechanics and quantum computing, respectively.

Let's start with quantum superposition. In quantum mechanics, superposition refers to the principle that any two (or more) quantum states can be added together, or "superposed", resulting in another valid quantum state. In a sense, the qubit, the fundamental unit of quantum information, can hold a state of both 0 and 1 simultaneously due to the principle of superposition. If we represent the quantum state mathematically, it can be written as:

$$|\psi\rangle = \alpha|0\rangle + \beta|1\rangle$$

Here, $|\psi\rangle$ is a quantum state and $|0\rangle, |1\rangle$ are basis vectors. Also, α and β are complex coefficients of the basis vectors and satisfy $|\alpha|^2 + |\beta|^2 = 1$.

Quantum parallelism, on the other hand, is a key feature of quantum computing. It's the concept that a quantum computer can perform multiple calculations simultaneously. This comes from the property of a quantum system, in which a group of qubits can exist in a superposition of states, and computations can be done on all these possible states at once.

To illustrate, suppose you have a quantum system of n qubits. A system of n qubits in a classical computer has 2^n possible states, but it can only be in one of these states at any time. Conversely, in quantum computing, due to quantum superposition, a system of n qubits can represent all these 2^n states simultaneously. Here's an equation for quantum parallelism:

$$\prod_{j=1}^{n}(|0\rangle_j + |1\rangle_j) = |0\rangle_1|0\rangle_2 \dots |0\rangle_n + \dots + |1\rangle_1|1\rangle_2 \dots |1\rangle_n$$

In a nutshell, the relation between superposition and quantum parallelism is that superposition allows multiple computations at once on a quantum computer and this is what we refer to as Quantum Parallelism. Thus, quantum parallelism is the result of superposition within the context of computation. Superposition allows a quantum computer to process a significantly large number of combinations of states at once, granting it a potentially immense computational power.

2.8   How is the concept of superposition represented mathematically?

In quantum mechanics, the concept of superposition is represented by the principle of linear superposition, which is a fundamental axiom of quantum states. Mathematically, it states that if $|\psi 1\rangle$ and $|\psi 2\rangle$ are two possible states of a quantum system, then any linear combination of those states are also possible states.

Suppose we have a quantum state $|\psi 1\rangle$ and another quantum state $|\psi 2\rangle$. The superposition state of these states can be written as:

$$|\psi\rangle = \alpha|\psi 1\rangle + \beta|\psi 2\rangle$$

where $|\alpha|^2 + |\beta|^2 = 1$.

Here, and are complex probability amplitudes and can be any complex numbers. When squared ($|\alpha|^2$ and $|\beta|^2$), they give the probability of the quantum system being in the corresponding state. Therefore, if you were to measure this system, there is a $|\alpha|^2$ probability of the system being in state $|\psi 1\rangle$, and a $|\beta|^2$ probability of it being in state $|\psi 2\rangle$.

It's important to note that quantum superposition is fundamentally different from classical probability, because the coefficients and are complex numbers, allowing for interference effects. These effects can only be predicted by quantum mechanics.

2.9 How does superposition contribute to the potential power of quantum computing?

The concept of superposition in quantum mechanics is one of the core reasons why quantum computers could potentially outperform classical computers. In classical computers, information is processed in binary units called bits, which can exist in one of two states at any one time: 0 or 1.

However, quantum bits (qubits) utilise the properties of quantum mechanics, such as superposition, to exist in multiple states simultaneously.

A qubit, unlike a classical bit, can exist in a state that is a superposition of both 0 and 1, represented as $|\psi\rangle = \alpha|0\rangle + \beta|1\rangle$, where and are complex numbers, and $|\alpha|^2$ and $|\beta|^2$ correspond to the probabilities of the qubit collapsing into the states $|0\rangle$ and $|1\rangle$ respectively.

If we had a quantum computer with 'n' qubits in superposition, in theory, we could perform calculations on 2^n states simultaneously, where 'n' is the number of qubits used. So, for example, a 2-qubit system could perform a computation on 4 states simultaneously, a 3-qubit system on 8 states, and so forth. Therefore, as the number of qubits grows, the increased capacity for simultaneous computation grows exponentially, not linearly as with classical computers. This leads to a tremendous increase in computational power.

Let's consider a simple representation for 2 qubits:

$$|00\rangle = 1|00\rangle + 0|01\rangle + 0|10\rangle + 0|11\rangle$$
$$|01\rangle = 0|00\rangle + 1|01\rangle + 0|10\rangle + 0|11\rangle$$
$$|10\rangle = 0|00\rangle + 0|01\rangle + 1|10\rangle + 0|11\rangle$$
$$|11\rangle = 0|00\rangle + 0|01\rangle + 0|10\rangle + 1|11\rangle$$

But unlike classical bits, qubits can exist in any superposition of these states, such as:

$$|\psi\rangle = 0.2|00\rangle + 0.3|01\rangle + 0.1|10\rangle + 0.4|11\rangle$$

In this example, the probabilities of the outcomes 00, 01, 10, and 11 are 0.04, 0.09, 0.01, and 0.16, respectively.

However, superposition is more than just an expansion of possibilities. It redefines how information is stored and manipulated, leading to quantum algorithms that solve certain problems more efficiently than classical algorithms. Examples include Shor's algorithm for factorization and Grover's algorithm for searching.

Please note that the manipulations of these superpositions in a controlled way are challenging and is a subject of current research in realizing practical quantum computers.

2.10 Can you provide an example of a quantum operation that uses superposition?

The superposition principle states that any quantum state can be represented as a sum, or a superposition, of two basis states. For a single qubit, these basis states are usually selected as $|0>$ (read as "ket 0") and $|1>$ (read as "ket 1").

The Hadamard gate creates superpositions when acting on qubits. Here's the matrix representation of the Hadamard gate:

$$H = \frac{1}{\sqrt{2}} \begin{bmatrix} 1 & 1 \\ 1 & -1 \end{bmatrix}$$

Let's see what the Hadamard gate does to the basis states.

1. When it acts on the state $|0>$, it generates the state $(|0> + |1>)/\text{sqrt}(2)$. In terms of the Bloch sphere representation, you started from the north pole and ended up on the equator (say, the point facing you).

$$H|0\rangle = \frac{1}{\sqrt{2}} \begin{bmatrix} 1 & 1 \\ 1 & -1 \end{bmatrix} \begin{bmatrix} 1 \\ 0 \end{bmatrix} = \frac{1}{\sqrt{2}} \begin{bmatrix} 1 \cdot 1 + 1 \cdot 0 \\ 1 \cdot 1 - 1 \cdot 0 \end{bmatrix} = \frac{1}{\sqrt{2}} \begin{bmatrix} 1 \\ 1 \end{bmatrix} = \frac{1}{\sqrt{2}}(|0\rangle + |1\rangle)$$

2. When it acts on the state $|1>$, it generates the state $(|0> - |1>)/\text{sqrt}(2)$. From the Bloch sphere perspective, you started from the south pole and, again, ended up on the equator, but at the diametrically opposed point from the previous one.

$$H|1\rangle = \frac{1}{\sqrt{2}} \begin{bmatrix} 1 & 1 \\ 1 & -1 \end{bmatrix} \begin{bmatrix} 0 \\ 1 \end{bmatrix} = \frac{1}{\sqrt{2}} \begin{bmatrix} 1 \cdot 0 + 1 \cdot 1 \\ 1 \cdot 0 - 1 \cdot 1 \end{bmatrix} = \frac{1}{\sqrt{2}} \begin{bmatrix} 1 \\ -1 \end{bmatrix} = \frac{1}{\sqrt{2}}(|0\rangle - |1\rangle)$$

The above equations show that the Hadamard gate creates a superposition of the states |0> and |1>.

The resulting states are said to be in superposition because we typically cannot say in which of the basis states the system is before we make a measurement. The measurement will 'force' the system to 'choose' one of the basis states, and we can only predict the probability of the outcome. Before the measurement, the system can be considered to be in all of its possible states at once, with the probability of each state defined by its corresponding amplitude.

2.11 How does quantum entanglement work, and why is it so fundamental to quantum mechanics?

Quantum Entanglement is a very peculiar and fundamental phenomenon of Quantum Mechanics. It occurs when two or more particles become linked, and the state of one particle can instantly influence the state of the other, no matter how far apart they are. This interconnectedness has been described as "spooky action at a distance" by Albert Einstein.

This is fundamentally different from any classical physical laws we know. The way these particles become 'entangled' is that they somehow become instantaneously connected to each other. Be that they originate from the same source or they interacted physically somewhere along the line. But once they've been entangled, the two particles become correlatively linked.

Let's look at a simple theoretical example using the basics concept of Quantum Mechanics, spin states. Consider two electrons which are formed in a singlet state, this means their combined spin must be 0. Individually, these electrons have "spin up" (+1/2) or "spin down" (-1/2) states. If you measure one and discover it in a "spin up" state, quantum entanglement means you instantly know the other one will be in the "spin down" state and vice versa, regardless of the distance between them.

The mathematical representation of an entangled state of two spins can be as follows:

$$|\Psi\rangle = \frac{1}{\sqrt{2}} \left(|+\rangle_1 |-\rangle_2 - |-\rangle_1 |+\rangle_2 \right)$$

where $|+\rangle$ and $|-\rangle$ denote "spin up" and "spin down" states respectively, and the subscripts 1 and 2 denote the two different particles.

It is important to note that the outcome is not determined until the measurement is made. This is a direct result of the principle of superposition in quantum mechanics, where a physical system such as these electrons exist in all its theoretically possible states simultaneously, but when measured or observed, it gives a result corresponding to only one of the possible configurations.

The reason why quantum entanglement is so fundamental to quantum mechanics is because it strikes at the core of what quantum mechanics is all about - being a nonlocal theory, coherence, and superposition of quantum states. Solutions to the equations of Quantum Mechanics are wave functions, which can be spread out over space and time. In other words, one part of the system might very well "know" about changes to another part of the system instantaneously.

Quantum entanglement has very active applications in Quantum Information Science, such as quantum computing and quantum cryptography. In Quantum Computing, quantum bits (qubits) can be entangled to enrich computational capacity through superposition and entanglement, while quantum cryptography uses entanglement to ensure security by enabling the detection of eavesdropping.

2.12 What are Bell states, and how do they illustrate the concept of entanglement?

Bell states, named after physicist John Stewart Bell, are specific quantum states of two qubits that represent the simplest examples of quantum entanglement. Quantum entanglement is a quantum mechanical phenomenon in which the quantum states of two or more objects have to be described with reference to each other, even though the individual objects may be spatially separated.

There are four Bell states:

1. $|\Phi^+\rangle = \frac{1}{\sqrt{2}}(|0,0\rangle + |1,1\rangle)$

2. $|\Phi^-\rangle = \frac{1}{\sqrt{2}}(|0,0\rangle - |1,1\rangle)$

3. $|\Psi^+\rangle = \frac{1}{\sqrt{2}}(|0,1\rangle + |1,0\rangle)$

4. $|\Psi^-\rangle = \frac{1}{\sqrt{2}}(|0,1\rangle - |1,0\rangle)$

Each Bell state is a superposition of two basis states, and the coefficients related to the states are complex numbers.

The Bell states exhibit properties of quantum entanglement. In a Bell state, if you measure one qubit, you will instantly know the state of the other, regardless of the distance that separates them. This is known as quantum correlation.

For example, in the Bell state $|\Phi^+\rangle$, if you measure one of the qubits and find it in state $|0\rangle$, you immediately know that the other qubit must also be in state $|0\rangle$. Likewise, if the first qubit is in state $|1\rangle$, the second is also in state $|1\rangle$.

This shows that the two qubits are not independent, even though they might be spatially separated. Their states are 'entangled', which marks a profound departure from classical physics.

2.13   Can you explain the concept of "spooky action at a distance" in quantum entanglement?

Let's first begin with a bit of context. The term "spooky action at a distance" is often used to describe quantum entanglement, and it was coined by Albert Einstein, who was famously uncomfortable with this aspect of quantum mechanics.

Quantum entanglement refers to a physical phenomenon where pairs or groups of particles become linked, such that the state of one particle cannot be described independently of the state of the other, even when particles are separated by large distances.

Now to the concept in detail:

Consider two particles A and B that are entangled. This means, if we describe the system, we must describe it as a whole. They lose their individual descriptions. So, let's assume A and B are in an entangled state $|\psi\rangle$, described by the equation:

$$|\psi\rangle = \frac{1}{\sqrt{2}}(|0_A\rangle|0_B\rangle + |1_A\rangle|1_B\rangle)$$

In this state either both are in the state 0 or both in the state 1. But neither of them possesses a definite state by itself.

Now, when we measure A to be in state 0, due to the quantum correlation, we'll know that B must also be in state 0. This is where Einstein's "spooky action at a distance" comes in, as B's state instantly collapses to 0 despite any potential distance between the particles A and B. This has even been experimentally verified in what are called Bell test experiments.

The 'spooky' part is that no 'local realist' theory, where influences are restricted to travel at the speed of light, could explain these quantum correlations. Thus, either locality – the principle that objects can only be influenced by their immediate surroundings – or realism – the principle that particles have definite properties even when not being measured – or both must be given up to accommodate quantum mechanics.

It's important to note that while quantum entanglement allows for this instantaneous correlation across distances, it does not allow for faster-than-light communication, as the resultant state from the collapse cannot be chosen, rather it is fundamentally random.

Quantum entanglement is still being researched extensively today, and has formed the basis for quantum information science and quantum computing technology.

2.14 How does entanglement contribute to the power of quantum computing?

Quantum entanglement is a key pillar in quantum computing and constitutes a central part of the extraordinary power that is inherent in quantum systems. At its core, entanglement is a unique quantum phenomenon that occurs when pairs or groups of particles interact in such a way that the quantum state of each individual particle is dependent on the state of the others, no matter how far apart they are. This peculiar property allows quantum bits (qubits) to be correlated in ways that are profoundly dissimilar from classical bits, giving rise to a massive increase in computing power when compared to classical computers.

The origins of entanglement's computational power draw from an interpolation of two central advantages.

1. Superposition: Quantum bits (qubits) can exist in a state of superposition, where they are not just in a state of '0' or '1' (like classical bits), but they can also be in a state that is a combination of both the states.

2. Entanglement: When qubits are entangled, the information of one qubit will immediately affect the other, no matter how far apart they are.

Given a set of N qubits, a classical computer could represent and manipulate an arbitrary state in 2^N complex dimensions. Quantum computers, however, can represent and manipulate all 2^N combinations at once, thanks to entanglement and superposition. This exponential growth in the number of states we can simultaneously consider gives rise to the phenomenal processing potential of quantum computers.

For instance, consider a system of 3 qubits. Without entanglement, a quantum computer could only ever manipulate 8 (2^3) states one at a time. With entanglement, however, this system potentially has access to all 8 states simultaneously. Essentially, the system can perform a computation on all 8 states in just one step.

In conclusion, entanglement provides a vast computational resource due to its ability to manipulate larger state spaces and conduct concurrent computations on all enumerable states at once. It is one of the reasons quantum computing, if scaled appropriately, has the potential to outperform classical computing on various complex problems including factorization, database searching, and simulation of quantum systems.

2.15 Can you provide an example of a quantum operation that uses entanglement?

Quantum entanglement is an essential feature of quantum computing which allows us to create highly correlated quantum states. A well-known quantum operation which uses entanglement is known as an "Entangling Gate."

The two-qubit Controlled-NOT gate (CNOT gate) is a common example of an entangling gate, which entangles two qubits together. The mechanism of operation is as follows: if the control qubit is in state $|1\rangle$, it will flip the target qubit, if the control qubit is in state $|0\rangle$, it will leave the target qubit alone.

To express this more formally, let's assume the control qubit is q_1 and the target qubit is q_2. The operation matrix of the CNOT gate in the computational basis $(|00\rangle, |01\rangle, |10\rangle, |11\rangle)$ is:

$$CNOT = \begin{pmatrix} 1 & 0 & 0 & 0 \\ 0 & 1 & 0 & 0 \\ 0 & 0 & 0 & 1 \\ 0 & 0 & 1 & 0 \end{pmatrix}$$

Consider the following superposition state as an input state which is a product state (not entangled):

$$|\psi\rangle = \frac{1}{\sqrt{2}}(|0\rangle + |1\rangle) \otimes |0\rangle = \frac{1}{\sqrt{2}}(|00\rangle + |10\rangle)$$

Applying the CNOT gate to this state, we get:

$$CNOT|\psi\rangle = \frac{1}{\sqrt{2}}(|00\rangle + |11\rangle)$$

This final state is an example of a maximally entangled Bell state. It cannot be separated into a product state anymore, and changes to one qubit instantaneously affect the other, no matter how far apart they are. This is a direct effect of the CNOT gate, proving it as an entangling gate.

This concept is central to quantum computing and forms the underlying protocol for quantum teleportation and superdense coding.

2.16 What is quantum teleportation, and how does it work?

Quantum teleportation is a protocol in quantum information science that enables the transfer of quantum information from one location to another, without the physical transportation of the actual quantum system carrying the information. The name is a bit misleading, as it suggests the teleportation of matter from one place to another, while in reality it is the information that is being teleported. Quantum teleportation is primarily used in the field of quantum computing and quantum communication.

Let us break down the quantum teleportation process:

1. **Entanglement**: The prerequisite for quantum teleportation is quantum entanglement, a unique quantum mechanical property that allows particles to correlate their states instantaneously, irrespective of the distance between them. If two particles are entangled, they are described by a single wave function, and a measurement on one particle immediately affects the state of the other. Suppose we have two entangled qubits, A and B, held by Alice and Bob respectively. The combined state can be written as:

$$|\Psi\rangle = \frac{1}{\sqrt{2}}(|00\rangle + |11\rangle)$$

2. **Alice's Measurement**: Alice wants to teleport the state of another qubit Q, i.e., $|\psi\rangle = \alpha|0\rangle + \beta|1\rangle$. She performs a Bell measurement on Q and her part of the entangled pair (qubit A). The Bell measurement is a projective measurement which projects the state of a pair of qubits into one of the Bell states (also known as EPR pairs).

3. **Communication**: Alice sends the result of her measurement (2 classical bits) to Bob through a classical communication channel.

4. **Bob's Transformation**: Depending on the message from Alice, Bob performs a suitable unitary transformation on his qubit (B).

The transformation maps his qubit into the state that Alice wanted to teleport - $|\psi\rangle = \alpha|0\rangle + \beta|1\rangle$.

The critical point to understand here is that no information is travelling faster than light (which would violate causality and hence the special theory of relativity) as the classical communication step cannot be faster than light. However, once the classical communication takes place, the state transfer is completed instantaneously.

Quantum teleportation is a fundamental quantum protocol and forms the backbone of many other protocols and algorithms in quantum information theory. Though we are still surrounding the practical implementation of quantum teleportation due to technological barriers, the quantum teleportation experiments with photons have been successfully conducted and are promising for future quantum technologies.

2.17 How does quantum teleportation differ from classical information transfer?

Quantum teleportation is far different from classical information transfer in several significant ways, primarily because the principles of quantum mechanics are fundamentally different from those of classical physics.

1. **Uncertainty & Non-cloning theorem:** Quantum states are subject to the Heisenberg uncertainty principle, which says it's impossible to copy an unknown quantum state. This is the "no-cloning" theorem in quantum mechanics. In classical information transfer, it's possible to make an exact copy of the information. That's also how we check for errors in data transmission.

2. **Entanglement:** Quantum teleportation relies on the phenomenon of quantum entanglement, where two particles become correlated in

such a way that the state of one instantly influences the state of the other, regardless of the distance between them. Entanglement isn't a feature of classical information transfer.

3. **Transmission of Information:** In classical systems, information moves from point A to point B. In contrast, in quantum teleportation, quantum information can be transferred from one place to another without physical transmission of the information carrier.

4. **Instantaneous Transfer:** Quantum teleportation allows for instantaneous transfer of information, irrespective of the distance. Classical information transfer, on the other hand, is bound by the speed of light.

It's important to note though that quantum teleportation is not about teleporting physical objects, but is about the transfer of information. It's a common confusion due to the term teleportation.

A simple diagram of quantum teleportation process can be visualized as:

```
Alice (source) --> (Quantum entanglement) --> Bob (destination)
```

Alice and Bob share an entangled pair of particles. Alice performs Bell-state measurement on her particle and the one to be teleported, causing her particle to collapse into one out of four possible states (00, 01, 10, 11). She sends the result to Bob (through classical channel) who uses this information to transform his entangled particle into the state that Alice wanted to teleport.

Also, remember the information teleportation is "destructive". The particle at Alice's side is no more in the state it was initially, meaning once teleported, the original quantum state no longer exists. This underscores the difference between teleportation and copying.

2.18   What is the role of entanglement in quantum teleportation?

Entanglement plays a vital role in quantum teleportation. It is what allows distinct quantum systems to be connected in such a way that the state of one directly affects the state of the other, no matter the distance between them.

To start, quantum entanglement is a quantum phenomenon where two or more particles become linked and the state of one particle is immediately connected to the state of the other, irrespective of the distance separating them. This was famously described by Albert Einstein as "Spooky Action at a Distance".

Quantum teleportation is the process by which the state of a qubit (the basic unit of quantum information) can be transmitted from one location to another, without the physical transportation of the qubit itself. As physical qubits are difficult to transport while preserving their quantum information, this process is critical in quantum information science.

The role of entanglement in quantum teleportation can be described using the following steps:

1. Alice and Bob (the typical characters used to describe this process) share an entangled pair of qubits, where Alice owns one qubit and Bob the other.

2. Alice performs a Bell measurement on her part of the entangled pair and the qubit she wants to teleport, which has the effect of entangling these two.

3. The result of Alice's measurement is then sent to Bob via classical communication, which instructs Bob how to transform his entangled qubit to get it into the desired state.

So, the role of entanglement in quantum teleportation serves as the "bridge" or conduit through which the quantum information can "travel" from Alice to Bob. Despite the fact that it may seem like the information travels instantly, it's important to note that a classical communication channel is used, which binds the process by the speed of light and ensures no violation of special relativity occurs.

In essence, entanglement enables the teleportation of quantum states, and without this "linkage" between quantum particles, these states couldn't be so perfectly transmitted across space.

Let's denote $|\psi\rangle$ as the state of the qubit to be teleported, initial state of each entangled pair $|\Phi^+\rangle = \frac{1}{\sqrt{2}}(|00\rangle + |11\rangle)$, $\{|0\rangle, |1\rangle\}$ as the standard base states.

$$
\begin{aligned}
|\psi\rangle_A |\Phi^+\rangle_{BC} = \frac{1}{\sqrt{2}} (&\alpha|0\rangle_A |0\rangle_B |\psi\rangle_C \\
&+ \alpha|0\rangle_A |1\rangle_B X|\psi\rangle_C \\
&+ \beta|1\rangle_A |0\rangle_B Z|\psi\rangle_C \\
&+ \beta|1\rangle_A |1\rangle_B ZX|\psi\rangle_C)
\end{aligned}
$$

This equation represents the entire system after Alice has measured her two qubits in the Bell base. Once Alice sends her result to Bob via classical communication, Bob performs X or Z operations if necessary and recovers $|\psi\rangle$. This shows that entanglement serves as a key enabling resource in the process of quantum teleportation.

2.19   Can quantum teleportation be used to transport matter?

No, quantum teleportation cannot be used to transport matter.

Quantum teleportation refers to transferring quantum information, specifically, the quantum state of a system, from one location to another without direct transmission of that system itself. It is based on the principles of quantum entanglement and quantum superposition invoked in quantum mechanics.

While it may sound like something out of a science fiction novel, in reality, it is more akin to transmitting information, not physical matter. This concept has been experimentally realized with photons, atomic ensembles, ions, electrons and superconducting circuits.

In mathematical terms, if one could denote the quantum states of the system and the teleportee as $|\psi\rangle$ and $|\phi\rangle$ respectively, then through quantum teleportation, the state $|\psi\rangle$ will be destroyed in one location and an exact replica, $|\phi\rangle$, will be created in a different location. This might be more clear if represented in the form of an equation:

Quantum System Before Teleportation:

$$|\Psi_1\rangle = |\psi\rangle,$$

$$|\Psi_2\rangle = |\phi\rangle$$

Quantum System After Teleportation:

$$|\Psi_1\rangle = |\phi\rangle, \text{(state of } \psi \text{ is destroyed)},$$

$$|\Psi_2\rangle = |\psi\rangle \text{(identical state of } \psi \text{ is created)}$$

This is different from classical communication because the information is not being sent, but rather instantaneously appearing at the second location.

It's also important to note that no physical entity is being moved from one place to another. Therefore, the term "teleportation" may be a bit of a misnomer. A better way to understand quantum teleportation is as a kind of sophisticated communication process that uses entangled particles to transmit quantum information.

2.20   What are the potential applications of quantum teleportation?

Quantum teleportation has several potential applications across different domains. It's a fundamental technique for transmitting information in quantum communication and quantum computing systems. Here's a list of few notable applications:

1. **Quantum Computing**: Quantum teleportation could play a crucial role in quantum computing. It allows for the creation of highly interconnected quantum systems which can help increase the computational power of quantum computers. Efforts are already underway to build quantum networks based on fault-tolerant quantum computation. A core element of these networks is a protocol known as "quantum teleportation" which allows quantum states to be transferred from one location to another, without the physical transport of the system hosting the quantum state.

2. **Quantum Communication and Cryptography**: Quantum teleportation can be used to establish highly secure communication channels. By virtue of Heisenberg's Uncertainty Principle, any attempt at eavesdropping can be easily detected. Thus, it opens the door for Quantum Key Distribution (QKD) which is integral for quantum cryptography. By using quantum teleportation, it is possible to securely transmit a private key needed for conventional cryptography systems.

3. **Quantum Networking**: Quantum teleportation can be used to transmit quantum information over long distances faster than the speed of light, without altering or destroying the original state of the information. This would enable the creation of high-speed quantum networks which would be far more efficient than current classical networks.

4. **Quantum Metrology**: Quantum teleportation could also enhance precision measurements by "teleporting" the state of a system to a probe before making a measurement.

5. **Distributed Quantum Computing**: The ability to teleport quantum information reliably would enable distributed quantum computation, a form of parallel processing that shares quantum information across numerous small quantum computers, analogous to a quantum version of today's computer networks or cloud computing.

Here is a table summarizing the key applications of Quantum Teleportation.

Field	Application
Quantum Computing	Interconnectivity, Computational power
Quantum Communication	High-speed secure communication
Quantum Cryptography	Quantum Key Distribution
Quantum Networking	High-speed efficient quantum networks
Quantum Metrology	Precise measurements
Distributed Computing	Distributed Quantum Computation, Cloud Computing

It is important to note that Quantum teleportation and Quantum Mechanics are still an active and rapidly expanding field. We should expect more unexpected applications in the near future.

Chapter 3

Quantum Bits (Qubits)

Chapter three introduces us to Quantum Bits, or 'qubits', the cornerstone of quantum computing. We examine what qubits are, their unique properties, and how they play a pivotal role in quantum computing, pushing the boundaries of what's possible in information processing.

3.1 What's the difference between a qubit and a classical bit?

In classical computing, a bit is the basic unit of information. It could be either in one of two states: 0 or 1, and that's it. In a simple sense, you could think of a bit as a tiny switch that can either be off (0) or on (1).

In quantum computing, we use quantum bits, or qubits. Much like a classical bit, a qubit can be in a state of 0 or 1. However, due to the principles of quantum mechanics, a qubit can also exist in what we call a superposition of states. This means it can be simultaneously in states 0 and 1, with coefficients that determine the probability of finding the system in either state upon measurement.

Mathematically this is represented as:

$$|\psi\rangle = \alpha|0\rangle + \beta|1\rangle$$

Here, $|\psi\rangle$ represents the quantum state, α and β are complex numbers, and $|\alpha|^2$ and $|\beta|^2$ represent the probability of finding the qubit in $|0$ and $|1$ states respectively at the time of measurement, satisfying the following condition $|\alpha|^2 + |\beta|^2 = 1$.

Another key difference is in the concept of entanglement. In quantum mechanics, if two qubits are entangled, the state of one qubit is directly related to the state of the other. This property does not exist in classical bits.

Lastly, unlike classical bits which undergo operations deterministically, operations on qubits are probabilistic and the outcomes can only be determined by making a measurement, at which point they 'collapse' to one of the basis states.

To sumarize, here is a comparison:

Characteristic	Classical Bit	Quantum Bit (Qubit)
States	0 or 1	0 and 1
Dependencies between bits	Independent	Can be entangled
Operations	Deterministic	Probabilistic

These characteristics of qubits enable quantum computers to process a higher amount of information and perform certain tasks more efficiently than classical computers. However, it also makes performing operations on qubits and maintaining their state over time a significant challenge.

3.2 How do the states of a qubit correspond to computational power?

The computational power offered by quantum bits, or qubits, comes from their unique quantum states and the associated principles of superposition and entanglement.

A classical computing bit can be in one of two states: 0 or 1. A qubit, on the other hand, can be in a state of 0, 1, or any superposition of these states. This is mathematically represented as:

$$|\Psi\rangle = \alpha|0\rangle + \beta|1\rangle$$

Here, α and β are complex numbers. When a qubit is measured, it will be in the state $|0\rangle$ with probability $|\alpha|^2$ or it will be in the state $|1\rangle$ with probability $|\beta|^2$. Because the probabilities must sum to 1, we have the normalization condition, $|\alpha|^2 + |\beta|^2 = 1$.

So to correlate with computational power, let's consider a system of 'n' qubits. While a classical 'n'-bit computer can be in one of 2^n configurations at a time, a quantum computer can be in any superposition of these 2^n states. Therefore, it can theoretically process 2^n values simultaneously, providing a potentially massive increase in computational power.

Moreover, the power of qubits is also derived from quantum entanglement. When qubits are entangled, the state of one qubit is directly related to the state of another, no matter how far apart they are. This allows one qubit state to instantaneously affect another entangled qubit state, which allows highly efficient manipulation of information.

However, it's crucial to note that harnessing the computational power of qubits is a complex task. Maintaining superposition and entanglement is challenging due to decoherence, and error correction in quantum systems is a non-trivial problem. We are still in the early stages of building usable quantum computers.

3.3   What is the concept of "state collapse" in the context of qubits?

Quantum state collapse or wave function collapse in the context of qubits pertains to the change that occurs in the state of a qubit (which exists in a superposition of states) when a measurement is made. It is a crucial concept in the field of quantum mechanics and quantum computing.

A qubit, unlike a classical binary bit that can be either 0 or 1, can be in a state which represents 0, or a state which represents 1, or a state that represents both 0 and 1 simultaneously due to the principles of superposition. The qubit state is often denoted as:

$$|\psi\rangle = \alpha|0\rangle + \beta|1\rangle$$

where α and β are probability amplitudes and can in general both be complex numbers. The absolute squares of these amplitudes, $|\alpha|^2$ and $|\beta|^2$, give the probabilities for the qubit to be found in the respective states $|0\rangle$ and $|1\rangle$ upon measurement.

Before measurement, you'd say that the qubit is in a superposition of states. When you measure this qubit, it will randomly collapse into one of its basis states $|0\rangle$ or $|1\rangle$, according to the probabilities given by $|\alpha|^2$ and $|\beta|^2$. The state it collapses into becomes the state of the qubit, and subsequent measurements will always give the same result, until the qubit is manipulated further. This immediate and random 'jump' to a totally determined state is what is termed as "state collapse" or "wave function collapse".

3.4 How does quantum superposition influence the properties of a qubit?

The concept of quantum superposition is a fundamental characteristic of the quantum world and it exerts significant influence on the properties of a quantum bit (qubit), enabling it to have multi-state simultaneity unlike classical bits. Here's how quantum superposition shapes the properties of a qubit:

1. **Multiple Simultaneous States**: In classical computing, a bit can exist solely in one of two states: 0 or 1. However, a qubit, on the other hand, due to quantum superposition, can exist in a simultaneous superposition of states. It can be in state 0, or it can be in state 1, or it can be in a superposition of both. The state of a qubit can be written as:

$$|\psi\rangle = \alpha|0\rangle + \beta|1\rangle$$

where α and β are complex numbers, and $|\alpha|^2 + |\beta|^2 = 1$. In other words, due to superposition, a qubit can carry more information than a classical bit.

2. **Parallelism**: Superposition allows multiple calculations to be carried out at once because a qubit can exist in multiple states. Thus, a quantum computer with multiple qubits (say n qubits) can potentially handle 2^n computations concurrently, offering a huge speed up for some specific problems when compared to classical computers.

3. **Interference**: The superposition property enables quantum interference, a noteworthy phenomenon in quantum mechanics. This could be simply showcased by the well-known "Double-split experiment". Binary outcomes with positive interference will result in a higher probability while negative interference lower probability.

4. **State Entanglement**: Unlike classical bits, qubits can be in entangled states due to quantum superposition. In this case, the state of a qubit cannot be described independently of the state of

the other qubits, leading to global intertwined quantum states that differs from their local constituents. In entangled states, measuring one qubit has an immediate effect on the state of another, no matter how far apart they are.

An practical example of use of superpositions on a real quantum computer can be IBM's quantum experience platform, which lets you create quantum circuits and run them on simulations or real quantum computers.

The fundamental trick to computational speed up in any Quantum Algorithm is smart manipulation of these superpositions, with quantum gates, such that computations interfere constructively for correct results and destructively for wrong answers.

Therefore, superposition is truly what separates quantum computing from classical computing and can be exploited to construct powerful algorithms.

3.5 How does the principle of quantum entanglement work with qubits?

Quantum entanglement is a fundamental principle of quantum mechanics that allows two or more particles to be inextricably linked to each other, no matter how far apart they may be.

When it comes to qubits, the principle works similarly. You see, the state of a qubit can be either 0 or 1 similar to a classical bit. However, the quantum magic happens when we consider the superposition state where a qubit can exist either as a 0 or 1 or both, thanks to quantum mechanics.

In an entangled state of two qubits, the information about one qubit instantaneously influences the other, regardless of the distance separating them. This is often referred to as "spooky action at a distance". This is different from classical bits where flipping one bit does not affect the state of other bits.

An entangled state of two qubits can be represented as follows:

$$|\Phi\rangle = \alpha|00\rangle + \beta|11\rangle$$

Here, the coefficients α and β determine the probabilities of measuring the states $|00\rangle$ and $|11\rangle$ respectively, and the state cannot be factorized into a product of two individual qubit states.

When we measure one of the entangled qubits, we instantly know the state of the other qubit. If the measured qubit collapses to a $|0\rangle$ state, the other qubit will also collapse to a $|0\rangle$ state. Similarly, if the measured qubit collapses to a $|1\rangle$ state, the other qubit will collapse to a $|1\rangle$ state. This correlation is maintained no matter how far apart the qubits are.

Quantum entanglement is a vital resource in quantum computing and quantum information science, providing a fundamental means of transferring information between qubits in quantum teleportation, quantum cryptography and quantum error correction.

3.6 What is the Bloch sphere, and how does it represent a qubit?

The Bloch sphere is a three-dimensional geometric representation used in quantum computing to visualize the state of a single quantum bit, or a qubit. Named after Swiss physicist Felix Bloch, it allows us to view the complete state of a qubit — its magnitude and phase — at a single glance.

The Bloch Sphere is typically depicted as a unit 3-dimensional sphere. At any given time, the state of a qubit is represented as a point inside (including surface) the sphere.

A classical bit can only be in one of two states - 0 or 1. In contrast, a qubit is a linear superposition of these states. Using Dirac notation, this is represented as:

$$|\Psi\rangle = \alpha|0\rangle + \beta|1\rangle$$

Here, $|0\rangle$ and $|1\rangle$ represent the basis states, and α and β are complex numbers. These numbers determine the probability of the qubit collapsing to either of the basis states upon measurement. According that, $|\alpha|^2 + |\beta|^2 = 1$ must always hold true.

The Bloch sphere offers a convenient way to visualize this. The two basis vectors $|0\rangle$ and $|1\rangle$ are represented by points at the top (north pole) and bottom (south pole) of the sphere. Any superposition state of the qubit is then a point within or on the surface of this sphere.

Here, $|\Psi\rangle$ is shown as vector from origin (center) to the exterior point.

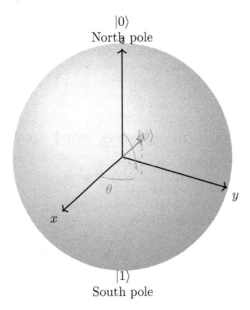

The angles θ and φ represent the probabilities and relative phase. The angle θ, between the z axis and the vector, is related to the probabilities of the basis states as $cos(\theta/2) = |\alpha|$ and $sin(\theta/2) = |\beta|$. The phase difference between the two states is represented by the angle φ in the x-y plane.

The Bloch Sphere is a powerful tool that helps to visualize the concepts of quantum superposition and phase, which are key to quantum computing.

3.7 How are operations on qubits represented geometrically using the Bloch sphere?

In Quantum Computing, the Bloch Sphere becomes an incredibly useful tool for visualizing qubit states and their transformations, as it provides for an appropriate geometric representation of qubit states. The sphere is named after the physicist Felix Bloch.

A qubit state is represented on the Bloch sphere as a point in three-dimensional space, as follows:

- A qubit in the state $|0\rangle$ is represented at the North Pole [0,0,1].

- A qubit in the state $|1\rangle$ is represented at the South Pole [0,0,-1].

- A qubit in superposition, defined as $\alpha|0\rangle + \beta|1\rangle$, can lie anywhere on the sphere.

Here, α and β are amplitude coefficients, with the stipulation that $|\alpha|^2 + |\beta|^2 = 1$, to ensure the qubit's state is correctly normalized.

Let's formulate these in terms of angles:

- $|0\rangle = cos(\theta/2)|0\rangle + sin(\theta/2)|1\rangle$,
- $|1\rangle = sin(\theta/2)|0\rangle - cos(\theta/2)|1\rangle$,

where θ is the angle made with the z-axis (the 'latitude'). The 'longitude' is represented by the azimuthal angle φ.

If we take these into account, a generalized state vector $|\psi\rangle$ can be represented as

$$|\psi\rangle = cos(\theta/2)|0\rangle + e^{i\varphi}sin(\theta/2)|1\rangle.$$

We can visualize quantum gates as operations that "rotate" the qubit state around the Bloch Sphere. For instance,

- The X-gate (Pauli-X) performs a π rotation of the qubit state around the x-axis.

- The Y-gate (Pauli-Y) does the same around the y-axis.

- The Z-gate (Pauli-Z) around the z-axis.

- The Hadamard gate acts by rotating by π about an axis lying the xy-plane (the line y=x).

- Phase shifts can be thought of as rotations around the z-axis.

Here are a few representative illustrations of operations on the Bloch sphere:

1. The Identity Gate (I): Leaves the qubit state unchanged (0 rotation).

2. The X-Gate (Pauli-X or NOT): Rotates the qubit state by π radians about the x-axis.

3. The Z-Gate (Pauli-Z or Phase-flip): Rotates the qubit state by π radians about the z-axis.

4. The Hadamard Gate (H): Rotates the qubit state by π radians around an axis lying in the xy-plane (the line y=x).

Understanding these principles gives us a tool to grasp the principles of quantum gates and their operations intuitively, beyond the dry formalisms of linear algebra.

3.8 What does it mean for qubits to be in a pure or mixed state?

In quantum mechanics, the state of a system is described by a state vector in a complex Hilbert space. The probabilities for different outcomes of measurements are given by the square of the absolute values of the vector's coefficients (the so-called Born rule). This leads to the two categories of quantum states: pure and mixed states.

1. Pure State:

A qubit is said to be in a pure state when it is described by a state vector in the Hilbert space. This means we have perfect knowledge of the quantum state. Formally, if $|\psi\rangle$ is the state of the system (where $|\psi\rangle$ is a normalized vector in the Hilbert space), then it's a pure state. For a qubit, this could look like $|\psi\rangle = a|0\rangle + b|1\rangle$, where a and b are complex numbers and $|a|^2 + |b|^2 = 1$. The numbers $|a|^2$ and $|b|^2$ are the probabilities of measuring the qubit in the states $|0\rangle$ and $|1\rangle$, respectively.

2. Mixed State:

A qubit is said to be in a mixed state when it is described by a statistical mixture of different pure states, equivalent to a density matrix. A mixed state represents a system where we do not have full knowledge of which particular states it can be in. The density matrix ρ is given by $\rho = \sum p_i |\psi_i\rangle \langle \psi_i|$ where the $|\psi_i\rangle$ are the possible pure states and the p_i are the probabilities of the system being in each state. Also, note that for a mixed state, the trace of ρ^2 is less than 1, while for a pure state, the trace of ρ^2 is exactly 1.

Mixed states often arise in quantum mechanics when a system is coupled to an environment, leading to phenomena such as decoherence.

For example, consider a qubit that is in a state $|0\rangle$ with probability $1/2$ and in state $|1\rangle$ with probability $1/2$; this would be considered a mixed state, as it is a statistical mixture of the two pure states $|0\rangle$

and $|1\rangle$.

3.9 What is the significance of the Pauli matrices in describing qubit operations?

The Pauli matrices play a significant role in describing qubit operations in quantum computing for two primary reasons: they provide a mathematical representation of quantum states, and they help describe state transformations or quantum gates.

These matrices, represented as X, Y, and Z, not only form a basis for the set of 2x2 Hermitian matrices, but also have distinctive properties such as they square to the identity, they are Hermitian, unitary, and moreover they have eigenvectors corresponding to the two possible outcomes of a measurement (i.e., $|0\rangle$ and $|1\rangle$ in quantum terminology for Z and X basses).

Let's denote them:

$$X = \begin{pmatrix} 0 & 1 \\ 1 & 0 \end{pmatrix}, \quad Y = \begin{pmatrix} 0 & -i \\ i & 0 \end{pmatrix}, \quad Z = \begin{pmatrix} 1 & 0 \\ 0 & -1 \end{pmatrix}$$

- The X-matrix, or Pauli-X gate, is a quantum gate that flips the state of a qubit from $|0\rangle$ to $|1\rangle$ or vice versa. It is the quantum equivalent of the NOT gate for classical computers and is sometimes referred to as a bit-flip.

- The Y-matrix, or Pauli-Y gate, is a combination of an X and a Z gate (up to a phase factor). It performs a bit and phase flip.

- The Z-matrix, or Pauli-Z gate, is a phase-flip gate, flipping the phase of a qubit if it's in state $|1\rangle$. This could be considered the quantum equivalent of a conditional NOT operation or it is called phase-flip gate.

These transformations can be used for various simple operations in a
quantum computer, and since any unitary operation can be decomposed into a multiple of simpler transformations, understanding how
Pauli matrices work is essential to understanding quantum computation.

3.10   How does quantum decoherence af-
fect qubit properties?

Quantum bits, or qubits, are fundamental to quantum computing.
A single qubit represents four potential states due to superposition
and entanglement, which absorbs quantum universal values 0 and 1
at the same time to create a subset of potential outputs that can be
calculated simultaneously.

However, Quantum decoherence can pose challenges to these properties. Quantum decoherence refers to the loss of quantum coherence.
In quantum mechanics, particles such as electrons behave equiva-
lently to waves and are described by a wavefunction. These waves
can interfere leading to the phenomenon of quantum interference and
superposition.

The 'decoherence' process attempts to destroy these quantum properties, leaving the qubits in a purely classical state, and thus removing
the core performance advantage of quantum computing. Specifically,
it does the following:

1) **Limits Superposition**: Quantum decoherence has the effect
of collapsing the superposition state of a qubit, thereby forcing it to
adopt a deterministic binary state. This severely limits the dimensional advantage of qubits over classical bits.

2) **Disengages Entanglement**: Quantum entanglement is a property which allows paired qubits to interact instantaneously regardless of distance. Quantum decoherence essentially disentangles these
qubits thereby affecting the speed and efficiency of quantum comput-

ing tasks.

3) **Increases Errors**: The process of quantum decoherence can introduce errors into quantum computing calculations. Given the delicate nature of quantum states, such errors can have a profoundly negative impact on the effectiveness of quantum computations.

Mathematically, the density matrix formalism is used to describe decoherence with respect to qubits. A quantum system in a pure state is described by a vector in a Hilbert space, while the decoherence implies the statistical mixtures of such states. Thus, the equation of motion for the density matrix under continuous observation is given:

$$\frac{d\rho}{dt} = -i[H, \rho] + \sum_k \left(V_k \rho V_k^\dagger - \frac{1}{2} \left\{ V_k^\dagger V_k, \rho \right\} \right)$$

Where ρ is the Density matrix, H is Hamiltonian operator governing the coherent evolution, V_k are operators that couple the system to the environment, and $\{,\}$ denotes the anti-commutator.

The second term on the right-hand side represents the decoherence; each V_k term can be seen as an error operator, describing a different kind of error depending upon its form.

Overall, maintaining the coherence of qubits is one of the major challenges in the development of quantum computers. Measures such as quantum error correction techniques and perfecting qubit insulation are some of the strategies used to minimize decoherence and harness the full benefits of quantum computing.

3.11   How do quantum gates operate on qubits?

Quantum gates, analogous to classical gates, operate on qubits by changing their states. However, unlike classical bits which are always in an either-or state (0 or 1), qubits can be in a superposition of states. Quantum gates manipulate these states, enabling the performance of computations that wouldn't be possible with classical computers.

A qubit is represented as a vector in a two-dimensional Hilbert space:

$$|\psi\rangle = \alpha|0\rangle + \beta|1\rangle$$

where $|\psi\rangle$ is the state of the qubit, $|0\rangle$ and $|1\rangle$ are the basis vectors, and   and   are complex numbers. The sum of the squares of the magnitudes of   and   equals 1. $|\alpha|^2$ gives the probability of the qubit being measured in state 0, and $|\beta|^2$ gives the probability of state 1.

Quantum gates apply linear, unitary transformations to these qubit states. One key characteristic of quantum gates is their reversibility – given the output, it is possible to recover the initial input.

Here are some key examples of quantum gates:

1. **Pauli-X gate**: Similar to a classical NOT gate. It flips the state of a qubit – $|0\rangle$ becomes $|1\rangle$ and vice versa. It's represented by the Pauli-X matrix:

$$X = \begin{bmatrix} 0 & 1 \\ 1 & 0 \end{bmatrix}$$

2. **Hadamard gate**: Produces a superposition of states from a single qubit. The state $|0\rangle$ is mapped to $\frac{|0\rangle+|1\rangle}{\sqrt{2}}$, and $|1\rangle$ is mapped to $\frac{|0\rangle-|1\rangle}{\sqrt{2}}$. The Hadamard gate is represented by the Hadamard matrix:

$$H = \frac{1}{\sqrt{2}} \begin{bmatrix} 1 & 1 \\ 1 & -1 \end{bmatrix}$$

3. **Pauli-Y and Pauli-Z gates**: Similar to the Pauli-X gate, these apply rotations around the Y and Z axes of the Bloch sphere. They're represented by the Pauli-Y and Pauli-Z matrices:

$$Y = \begin{bmatrix} 0 & -i \\ i & 0 \end{bmatrix}, Z = \begin{bmatrix} 1 & 0 \\ 0 & -1 \end{bmatrix}$$

4. **Controlled gates (e.g., CNOT)**: Apply a specified operation to one qubit (target) conditional on the state of another qubit (control). For example, in a CNOT gate, if the control qubit is in state $|1\rangle$, the target qubit is flipped.

These are just a few examples. There are many other types of quantum gates, including rotation gates, phase gates, Toffoli gates, and more. Like classical gates, quantum gates form the building blocks of quantum circuits, enabling complex quantum algorithms.

3.12   What is the role of measurement in manipulating qubits?

Measurement in quantum computing is a key process for information retrieval. Quantum systems are essentially probabilistic, and the act of measurement is when we extract definite information. This process is fundamentally different than in classical computational systems.

A classical bit is in one state of either 0 and 1. Unlike classical bits, a qubit can be in a superposition of states, meaning it can be in state $|0\rangle$, state $|1\rangle$, or any quantum superposition of these states:

$$|\Psi\rangle = \alpha|0\rangle + \beta|1\rangle$$

Here, $|\Psi\rangle$ represents the state of the qubit, and α and β are complex numbers. When we measure this qubit, we get either $|0$ with a probability $\|\alpha\|^2$ or $|1\rangle$ with a probability $\|\beta\|^2$. Here, $\|\alpha\|^2 + \|\beta\|^2 = 1$.

The second key difference from classical systems is that once a qubit is measured, the quantum state collapses to that particular state. This is known as wave function collapse. So, if we were in a superposition of states as given by $|\Psi\rangle$, after measurement, we will be left in a single state, either $|0\rangle$ or $|1\rangle$.

To illustrate these concepts, consider an example where a qubit is in state $|\Psi\rangle = \frac{1}{\sqrt{2}}|0\rangle + \frac{1}{\sqrt{2}}|1\rangle$. This indicates that the probabilities of measuring $|0\rangle$ and $|1\rangle$ are both $1/2$. If we measure this qubit and the outcome is $|1\rangle$, then, the state of the qubit immediately shifts to $|1\rangle$.

So, we see that measurement can seemingly "manipulate" the state of a qubit by forcing it into one of its basis states, but it's a fundamentally destructive process. It's also the only way we can extract classical information from a quantum computer, which is what makes quantum computing such a fascinating and challenging field.

3.13 How does entanglement between qubits contribute to the functioning of a quantum computer?

Entanglement is a fundamental aspect of quantum computing. It permits quantum bits or qubits to become interrelated in such a way that the state of each one is immediately connected with the state of the other, even when they are separated by large distances.

In terms of quantum computing, entanglement provides the computing power that distinguishes quantum computers from their classical counterparts. Two entangled qubits can represent and process four states simultaneously: $|00>$, $|01>$, $|10>$, and $|11>$. Here, the states are given as binary representations to provide an understanding in classical-computational terms.

This property scales exponentially with the number of qubits involved. For instance, 3 entangled qubits can represent $2^3 = 8$ states simultaneously, 4 qubits $2^4 = 16$ states, and so forth. If you have 'n' entangled qubits, you can simultaneously represent 2^n states.

This phenomenon gives quantum computers their intrinsic parallelism, allowing them to work on a million computations all at once, while a classical computer can only handle one.

Here is a tabela that shows the exponential scaling:

```
Qubits | States
   1   |   2
   2   |   4
   3   |   8
   4   |   16
   5   |   32
   n   |  2^n
```

Furthermore, entanglement allows for the establishment of quantum gates that involve more than a single qubit, which leads to the ability to construct more complex quantum circuits. For example, the CNOT gate (Controlled-NOT gate) in quantum computing acts on 2 qubits, changing the state of the second qubit (target qubit) if and only if the first qubit (control qubit) is in state $|1>$.

It's important to note that while entanglement provides significant computing power, the peculiar characteristics of entangled states also give rise to challenges in terms of error management and consistent quantum state maintenance, known as coherence.

In summary, entanglement is an essential resource in quantum computing because it underpins its exponential speed-up compared to classical computers, allows for complex multi-qubit operations, and permits intrinsic parallelism.

3.14   How is information encoded into qubits?

In classical computing, information is encoded into bits as binary values - 0 or 1.

Conversely, in quantum computing, information is encoded into quantum bits, or qubits. The fascinating and powerful aspect of quantum information is that a qubit can be in a state of 0, 1, or BOTH at the same time. This is a key principle of "superposition."

Before proceeding, it is essential to note that qubits are typically represented as quantum states in Hilbert space. They can be visually represented on a Bloch Sphere, which gives a better intuition of their actual state compared to just binary 1 or 0.

A generic qubit state $|\psi\rangle$ can be represented as:

$|\psi\rangle = \alpha|0\rangle + \beta|1\rangle$

The $|0\rangle$ and $|1\rangle$ represent the two basis states, analogous to binary values 0 and 1.

The α and β here are complex coefficients, and according to quantum mechanics, the absolute squares of these coefficients, $|\alpha|^2$ and $|\beta|^2$, give the probabilities of finding the qubit in the respective states upon measurement. As a result, qubits can represent a superposition of states until a measurement is made.

The encoding information into a qubit involves initializing it into a superposition state and utilizing quantum gates (analogous to classical gates in classical computing) to manipulate their states.

A good thing to note about encoding in quantum states is that due to the qubit's nature, information 'disturbs' the qubit - a characteristic known as Heisenberg's Uncertainty Principle. This property has powerful implications in data security and quantum cryptography.

Remember, the magic of quantum computing comes from this very property of qubits - to represent and manipulate multiple states at once, giving quantum computers their extraordinary computational power.

3.15   What does it mean to initialize a qubit, and why is this step important?

Initializing a qubit refers to the act of putting a qubit in a definite state. Most commonly, this is the state $|0\rangle$, which often means the qubit is in its ground state.

In the context of quantum mechanics, initialization is described by the equation:

$$|\psi\rangle = \alpha|0\rangle + \beta|1\rangle$$

where $|\psi\rangle$ is the state of our qubit, α and β are complex numbers, and their magnitudes squared describe the probability that a qubit, when observed, will be in state $|0\rangle$ or $|1\rangle$, respectively.

Initializing a qubit is fundamental because it establishes a known starting point for quantum computation or quantum information processing. Without a known or predictable initial state, the subsequent quantum processes may not be accurately controlled or predicted since the results of quantum computing operations are highly dependent on the initial state of the qubits. Similar to how classical computing bits are initialized to start processing digital information, quantum bits must also be initialized.

For example, in IBM's Quantum Experience, the initial state of every qubit in their processor is the ground state $|0\rangle$. A quantum circuit that hasn't done any operations merely measures each qubit in the state $|0\rangle$.

On the computational side also, it's important to note that if the quantum computer is considered as a multi-dimensional vector space, the initialization of a qubit to a particular initial state puts the system at a specific point in that multi-dimensional space. Each subsequent computational operation then involves transformations that move that point around in the vector space. Therefore, the starting point (i.e., the initialization) fundamentally affects the trajectory and the final result of the computation.

In most practical quantum computers, errors could also occur during the initialization process. That's why techniques such as quantum error correction and quantum fault tolerance are crucial, which consider the errors introduced during qubit initialization.

Chapter 4

Quantum Gates and Circuits

In the fourth chapter, we unravel the inner mechanics of quantum computation. We venture into the world of quantum gates and circuits, the basic architecture for performing quantum operations, providing a solid understanding of how quantum information is manipulated.

4.1 How do quantum gates differ from classical logic gates?

Quantum gates significantly differ from classical logic gates in a variety of ways.

1. **Superposition:** Quantum gates operate on quantum bits (or qubits) which can exist in a state of superposition of states. Unlike classical bits which can be either 0 or 1, qubits can be a superposition

of $|0\rangle$ and $|1\rangle$ states. This difference is fundamental as it introduces the uncertainty principle and allows us to create more powerful computing architectures.

2. **Unitarity:** Quantum gates must be unitary, this means that they represent reversible operations. Mathematically, an operator is called unitary if its inverse is equal to its Hermitian adjoint. This is in contrast with classical gates, which might not be reversible(e.g., AND, OR gates).

3. **Transformation:** Classical gates transform input bits to output bits deterministically. On the other hand, quantum gates transform quantum states to other quantum states through a probabilistic transformation, governed by the Schrödinger equation.

4. **Entanglement:** Quantum gates generate entangled states. Entanglement is a quantum phenomenon in which two or more particles become correlated in such a way that the state of one particle immediately influences the state of the other, no matter how far apart they are. This property is not present in classical gates.

All quantum gates can be represented by unitary matrices. For example, operation of a 'NOT' quantum gate (also known as Pauli-X gate), one of the most important single-qubit gates, on a quantum state can be represented as a matrix operation:

$$X = \begin{pmatrix} 0 & 1 \\ 1 & 0 \end{pmatrix}$$

If applied to a state $|0\rangle$, it yields $X|0\rangle = |1\rangle$, and if applied to a state $|1\rangle$, it yields $X|1\rangle = |0\rangle$. This is similar to how a classical 'NOT' gate works, but the superposition and entanglement properties differentiate it in a quantum context.

To visualize the sequence of quantum gates operation, we often use a quantum circuit. For example, a quantum circuit for a simple 'NOT' gate operation applied on a $|0\rangle$ state can be graphically represented as:

$$|0\rangle \ -\boxed{X}- \ |1\rangle$$

where '[X]' represents the Pauli-X gate. This depicts that the 'NOT' gate is applied on a $|0\rangle$ qubit, turning it into a $|1\rangle$ state.

4.2 What makes quantum gates reversible?

Quantum gates are reversible due to their inherent properties which can be traced back to the postulates of quantum mechanics. These postulates stipulate that a closed quantum system evolves according to a unitary transformation.

Unitary transformations are reversible - that is, they have an inverse. If a transformation U takes a state from $|\psi\rangle$ to $U|\psi\rangle$, there exists a transformation $U^\dagger$, known as the Hermitian conjugate (or sometimes referred to as the adjoint or the dagger) of U, which can take us back from $U|\psi\rangle$ to $|\psi\rangle$.

In matrix terms:
$$UU^\dagger = U^\dagger U = I$$
where U is a quantum gate (a unitary matrix), $U^\dagger$ is its Hermitian conjugate, and I is the identity matrix.

If we apply $U^\dagger$ immediately after applying U, the combined effect is just the identity operation, and we return to our original state. This is what makes quantum gates reversible.

Moreover, this property differentiates classical computing from quantum computing. Most classical gates (like AND, OR, NAND, etc.) are not reversible. For example, in the classical computing space, if you apply an AND gate on bit inputs and receive an output, you can't reverse engineer the input values just from the output. In contrast, quantum gates can always be 'undone' because every quantum gate has an inverse gate.

It's worth noticing that while quantum gates are reversible, measurements in quantum mechanics are not. Measuring a quantum state fundamentally changes the state, and there's no operation that can revert the system to a state before its measurement.

4.3 What are the Pauli gates, and how are they used in quantum circuits?

The Pauli gates or Pauli matrices are a set of three 2x2 matrices which are fundamental to quantum computing. They are used in the construction of quantum circuits to apply transformations to quantum bits (qubits). The Pauli gates are denoted by the symbols X, Y, and Z, each relating to rotation around the different axes of the Bloch sphere.

1. The X gate (also known as a bit-flip gate):

$$X = \begin{pmatrix} 0 & 1 \\ 1 & 0 \end{pmatrix}$$

An X gate applied to a qubit rotates the qubit's state around the X-axis of the Bloch sphere by π radians. It flips the state $|0\rangle$ to $|1\rangle$ and vice versa. It is identical to the NOT gate in classical computing.

2. The Y gate:

$$Y = \begin{pmatrix} 0 & -i \\ i & 0 \end{pmatrix}$$

The Y gate rotates the state of the qubit around the Y axis of the Bloch sphere by π radians.

3. The Z gate (also known as a phase-flip gate):

$$Z = \begin{pmatrix} 1 & 0 \\ 0 & -1 \end{pmatrix}$$

The Z gate rotates the state of the qubit around the Z axis of the Bloch sphere by π radians.

These operations induce quantum mechanical phenomena such as interference and entanglement, both of which are necessary for the operation of quantum algorithms and protocols. By using combinations of these gates in a quantum circuit, it's possible to fully control the quantum state of a register of qubits.

A sequence of Pauli gates on a quantum register prepares any possible configuration of quantum data, and it's possible to affect the amplitudes and phases of the quantum states. This is the foundation of universal quantum computation.

Note: Pauli matrices are Hermitian and Unitary, which maintains the norm of quantum states during operations. This is a crucial in quantum computing to ensure valid quantum states through quantum computation.

4.4 What is the significance of the Hadamard gate?

The Hadamard gate is a fundamental quantum gate in quantum computing. It is especially significant for its ability to create superposition states, which is a key aspect of quantum computations.

The Hadamard gate acts on a single qubit to create a superposition. It can transform a qubit that is in a definite state (either |0> or |1>) into a state of superposition. Specifically, the Hadamard transform maps the basis states as follows:

$$|0\rangle \rightarrow \frac{|0\rangle + |1\rangle}{\sqrt{2}}$$

$$|1\rangle \rightarrow \frac{|0\rangle - |1\rangle}{\sqrt{2}}$$

This results in the qubit being in a state that when measured, has a 50% chance of being in the state $|0>$ and a 50% chance of being in the state $|1>$.

Furthermore, applying the Hadamard gate twice in a row to a qubit brings the qubit back to its original state. That is, for any qubit state $|\psi>$, $H(H|\psi>) = |\psi>$.

The Hadamard gate, represented symbolically as "H", can be represented by the following 2x2 unitary matrix:

$$H = \frac{1}{\sqrt{2}} \begin{bmatrix} 1 & 1 \\ 1 & -1 \end{bmatrix}$$

Through the mechanism of superposition, the Hadamard gate reveals the power of quantum computing: the ability to be in multiple states simultaneously, which enables quantum algorithms to search through all possible solutions of a problem at the same time.

4.5   How is entanglement created using quantum gates like CNOT?

In quantum computing, entanglement is a special condition in which the pair or group of qubits, no matter how far apart they are, are linked in such a way that the quantum state of any one of them cannot be adequately described without full mention of its counterpart — even if the individual objects are spatially separated.

One particular quantum gate that can create such entanglement is the Controlled-NOT, or CNOT gate. The CNOT gate operates on two qubits and can create superposition or entanglement.

The representation of a CNOT gate is:

$$\begin{pmatrix} 1 & 0 & 0 & 0 \\ 0 & 1 & 0 & 0 \\ 0 & 0 & 0 & 1 \\ 0 & 0 & 1 & 0 \end{pmatrix}$$

As an example, let's use a CNOT gate on a simple system of two qubits. Let's assume the first qubit is in state $|0\rangle$ (in the X basis) and the second qubit is in state $|+\rangle = (|0\rangle + |1\rangle)/\sqrt{2}$ (in the Y basis). This means that our initial state could be represented as $|0+\rangle = |0\rangle|+\rangle$, where the first slot represents the control qubit and the second slot - the target.

Applying a CNOT gate changes the state of the second (target) qubit if the first (control) qubit is in state 1. Therefore, in our case, the state of the system remains unchanged since the control qubit's state is 0.

However, if we flip the control qubit to state $|1\rangle$ before applying the CNOT operation, then our state becomes $|1+\rangle = |1\rangle(|0\rangle + |1\rangle)/\sqrt{2} = 1/\sqrt{2} * (|10\rangle + |11\rangle)$. Now, the target qubit state will flip if control qubit is in state 1. Hence, our final state after applying CNOT gate would be: $1/\sqrt{2} * (|10\rangle + |11\rangle)$

This final state is an example of an entangled state. That is because the state of our two-qubit system cannot be separated into one qubit states. We can see that the state of the system is a superposition of the states in which the two qubits are either both 0 or both 1.

In general, the CNOT and similar quantum gates serve as fundamental building blocks for creating multi-qubit entangled states and for executing quantum algorithms. Therefore, understanding how these gates manipulate quantum states is crucial for advancing the field of quantum computing.

4.6 What is the purpose of the phase gate?

The Phase Gate (often represented as P or S) in Quantum Computing is one of the fundamental single-qubit gates. Its primary purpose is to introduce a phase change, effectively changing the state of a qubit without affecting its probability distributions when measured along the computational (Z) basis.

Mathematically, the Phase Gate operates on a single qubit $|\psi\rangle = \alpha|0\rangle + \beta|1\rangle$ to add a phase of ϕ (where ϕ is a real number) to the state $|1\rangle$ in a basis-independent manner (it does not change the state $|0\rangle$).

The operation of the phase gate is defined as:

$P|0\rangle = |0\rangle$

$P|1\rangle = e^{i\phi}|1\rangle$

In matrix form, the Phase Gate is represented as:

$$P = \begin{pmatrix} 1 & 0 \\ 0 & e^{i\phi} \end{pmatrix}$$

The P gate can be used as a building block for creating more complex gates, circuits, and algorithms in quantum computing. It essentially allows for the manipulation of phase information in quantum states, which can encode important quantum information and affects interference patterns–an essential component in many quantum algorithms (e.g. Quantum Phase Estimation, Quantum Fourier Transform).

Here's a basic example: The commonly used S gate (square root of Z gate) and T gate (a phase gate with $\phi = \pi/4$) are specific cases of the phase gate:

$$S = \begin{pmatrix} 1 & 0 \\ 0 & i \end{pmatrix}$$

$$T = \begin{pmatrix} 1 & 0 \\ 0 & e^{i\pi/4} \end{pmatrix}$$

Note that these minuscule transformations might seem irrelevant, but when combined and repeated over large quantum systems, they create significant changes, forming the basis of various quantum algorithms.

4.7 How is a Toffoli gate used in quantum computing, and why is it sometimes called a "universal" gate?

A Toffoli gate, also known as controlled-controlled-not (CCNOT), is a three-qubit gate in quantum computing. It applies a Pauli-X or NOT-gate to the third qubit (the target qubit) if the first two qubits (the control qubits) are both in the state $|1\rangle$.

The matrix representation of the Toffoli gate is:

$$CCNOT = \begin{bmatrix} 1 & 0 & 0 & 0 & 0 & 0 & 0 & 0 \\ 0 & 1 & 0 & 0 & 0 & 0 & 0 & 0 \\ 0 & 0 & 1 & 0 & 0 & 0 & 0 & 0 \\ 0 & 0 & 0 & 1 & 0 & 0 & 0 & 0 \\ 0 & 0 & 0 & 0 & 1 & 0 & 0 & 0 \\ 0 & 0 & 0 & 0 & 0 & 1 & 0 & 0 \\ 0 & 0 & 0 & 0 & 0 & 0 & 0 & 1 \\ 0 & 0 & 0 & 0 & 0 & 0 & 1 & 0 \end{bmatrix}$$

The Toffoli gate is often called a "universal gate" because it is reversible and can be used to construct any other logic gate. When we say a gate is "universal," it means that any computation can be implemented using combinations of that gate. Traditional digital computers are based on combinations of the NAND gate, which is a universal gate for classical digital circuits. In a similar way, any quantum computation can be constructed from a certain set of quantum gates.

More specifically, the Toffoli gate, along with the Hadamard gate (a single-qubit gate), is sufficient for universal quantum computation. This is because they form a universal gate set for the Clifford+T gate set, which includes the CNOT, Pauli, Hadamard, Phase, $\pi/8$ (a.k.a "T") gates, and their adjoints.

Note that despite being universal, it's often more efficient to use other gates depending on the specific problem and quantum hardware.

4.8 What is the controlled-Z (CZ) gate, and how is it used in quantum computing?

Controlled-Z (CZ) gate is a two qubit gate in quantum computing, having one control qubit and one target qubit. It's a crucial tool to perform quantum computational tasks because it provides a way to manipulate the phase of the state vector based on the state of the control qubit.

The matrix representation of the CZ gate is:

$$CZ = \begin{bmatrix} 1 & 0 & 0 & 0 \\ 0 & 1 & 0 & 0 \\ 0 & 0 & 1 & 0 \\ 0 & 0 & 0 & -1 \end{bmatrix}$$

The action of the CZ gate can be understood as follows: if the state of the control qubit is $|0\rangle$, the target qubit remains unchanged. But if the control qubit is in the state $|1\rangle$, then the sign of the target qubit is flipped (i.e., the phase of the state is rotated by π).

For a more visual representation, consider that we have two qubits in states $|\psi\rangle = \alpha|0\rangle + \beta|1\rangle$ (control) and $|\varphi\rangle = \gamma|0\rangle + \delta|1\rangle$ (target). If we apply the CZ gate to these states, the resultant states will be:

$CZ(|\psi\rangle, |\varphi\rangle) = (\alpha|0\rangle + \beta|1\rangle)(\gamma|0\rangle + (-\delta)|1\rangle)$, if the control qubit is $|1\rangle$.

$CZ(|\psi\rangle, |\varphi\rangle) = (\alpha|0\rangle + \beta|1\rangle)(\gamma|0\rangle + \delta|1\rangle)$, if the control qubit is $|0\rangle$.

CZ gate is widely used in quantum algorithms, for instance, it forms an integral part in the creation of entangled states and it's particularly used in quantum error correction, quantum teleportation, and quantum algorithm design such as the quantum phase estimation algorithm. Its ability to flip the phase of the state vector introduces useful computational possibilities in manipulating and creating new states.

4.9 What role does the SWAP gate play in quantum algorithms?

The SWAP gate in quantum computing is a two-qubit operation that exchanges the quantum states of two qubits. In other words, if the two qubits are in states $|a\rangle$ and $|b\rangle$ respectively, the SWAP gate will result in the qubits being in states $|b\rangle$ and $|a\rangle$.

In a quantum computing system, when qubits interact with each other during quantum computing operations, they typically have to be situated very close to one another. In other words, if a specific algorithm requires qubits in non-neighboring positions to interact, then some mechanism is needed to facilitate this interaction. This is where the SWAP gate comes into the picture.

For example, let's consider a three-qubit quantum circuit that's initially in state $|abc\rangle$. We could use two SWAP gates to switch the states of the first qubit and the third qubit as follows:

Here 'x' represents the SWAP gate.

In the context of quantum algorithms, the SWAP gate is a useful tool as it allows us to "move" quantum information around in our quantum system. This can be crucial for implementing certain quantum algorithms, where we may need to control the interactions between qubits that are not immediately adjacent to each other.

Note that a SWAP gate can be composed of three CNOT gates as follows:

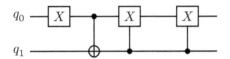

where the 'X' represents a CNOT gate. This is important for physical implementation on quantum devices which might not natively support a SWAP operation, but do support the CNOT operation.

Moreover, since gates are error-prone in a quantum computer, having a large number of SWAP gates to implement in a quantum system may cause a quantum algorithm to be less accurate. Hence it's always crucial to minimize the use of SWAP gates and to include them only when necessary.

4.10 How does a quantum Fourier transform (QFT) gate work, and why is it important?

The Quantum Fourier Transform (QFT) is analogous to the Discrete Fourier Transform (DFT) in classical computing but it operates on quantum bits (qubits). The QFT allows quantum computers to transform states in a way that can reveal key data about a quantum system, such as the periodicity of a function. For a state made up of "n" qubits where $n > 1$, the QFT is a linear transformation that transforms these quantum states according to the formula:

$$|j\rangle \rightarrow \frac{1}{\sqrt{N}} \sum_{k=0}^{N-1} e^{2\pi i jk/N} |k\rangle \quad \text{for } j = 0, ..., N-1$$

where $N = 2^n$.

The importance of QFT lies in its ability to transform the quantum states to a basis where the information we seek (like phase or frequency) becomes easy to extract. It is a crucial component of many important quantum algorithms such as Shor's algorithm for integer factorization, and the quantum phase estimation algorithm. These algorithms demonstrate a significant quantum speedup over the best-known classical algorithms.

To operate the QFT on a quantum circuit, it needs to be decomposed into a sequence of basic quantum gates such as Hadamard gates and controlled phase rotations. This gate sequence starts from the Most Significant Qubit (MSQ), so it is a highly parallel process. Here is the schematic diagram for a 3-qubit QFT:

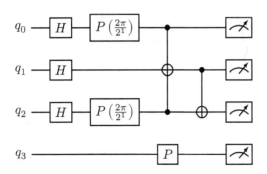

In this circuit, 'P' represents a phase rotation gate, 'H' represents the Hadamard gate, the ' ' symbol represents controlled-'P' gates, and 'M' represents a measurement. The controlled phase rotations enable the interference effects that are crucial to the QFT, turning the relative phases between different states into relative probabilities which can be read out with a measurement.

The crucial step in the circuit is the swaps at the end of the circuit. These are necessary because the QFT outputs the qubits in reverse order, so if we want the MSB to be on the top, we need to swap the qubits.

However, in actual implementation in quantum computer or simulation, these swaps can be ignored by reversing the output string.

4.11 How are quantum circuits structured, and how do they differ from classical circuits?

Quantum circuits are structured to take advantage of the principles of quantum mechanics in order to perform computation. Like classical circuits, quantum circuits consist of wires and logical gates. However, there are some crucial differences between the two due to the nature of quantum bits (qubits) as opposed to classical bits.

1. **Superposition**: Classical bits are binary, meaning they can be in one of two states: 0 or 1. Qubits, on the other hand, can be in a state of superposition of 0 and 1, meaning they can be in both states at once. This is often represented as follows, where   and   are complex numbers:

$$|\Psi\rangle = \alpha|0\rangle + \beta|1\rangle$$

2. **Entanglement**: While the state of a classical bit is independent of the states of all other bits, qubits can be entangled. This means that the state of one qubit is dependent on the state of another, no matter how far apart they are.

3. **Reversibility**: Quantum gates are reversible, which is not generally the case with classical gates. This means the input state can be recovered if the output state is known.

4. **Unitarity**: Quantum gates are represented by unitary operators, which preserve the total probability when a state is transformed.

The structure of a quantum circuit is generally represented as a sequence of quantum gates (each acting on one or two qubits) that operate on an initial state of qubits. The rows represent qubits and columns represent operations on these qubits. The operations are applied from left to right.

As an example, here is the circuit for the CNOT (Controlled NOT) gate, a fundamental two-qubit gate:

Here, the ● symbol represents the control qubit and the ⊕ symbol represents the target qubit. This operation flips the target if the control is set to $|1\rangle$. These gate diagrams are a graphical representation of the unitary matrices that describe the quantum operations.

In terms of the differences with classical circuits, the superposition principle allows quantum circuits to potentially perform many computations simultaneously, which is the basis for the potential speed-up of quantum computers. Entanglement allows qubits to be correlated in ways that are not possible for classical bits, providing another resource for quantum computation. The reversibility of quantum gates means that quantum computation does not have to dissipate energy in the same way that classical computation does.

4.12 What does it mean to measure a quantum circuit?

Measurement in the context of quantum circuits is a fundamental concept in quantum computing which deeply highlights the differences between the classical computation and the quantum computation.

In classical computing, measuring or observing the state of a system, say a bit, is simply reading off its state, which could be either 0 or 1. Importantly, this measurement process does not disturb the system.

Conversely in quantum computing, measurement of a quantum state (called a qubit in quantum computing) is not that straightforward and nondestructive. This comes from the fundamental principles of quantum mechanics - Heisenberg Uncertainty Principle and the principle of superposition.

1. **Superposition Principle**: In quantum computing, a qubit could exist not just in state $|0>$ or $|1>$ (denotations for the binary states), but also in superpositions of both. Meaning, a quantum system can be in multiple states at the same time. This is represented by coefficients (complex numbers) 'a' and 'b' for each state as:

$$|\psi\rangle = a|0\rangle + b|1\rangle$$

where $|a|^2$ and $|b|^2$ are the probabilities of the system being in state $|0>$ or $|1>$, respectively.

2. **Measurement or Observation**: When we measure a quantum system, it 'collapses' from its superposition state to one of its basis states ($|0>$ or $|1>$). This collapse is probabilistic and it would collapse to say $|0>$ with probability $|a|^2$ and to $|1>$ with probability $|b|^2$.

3. **Heisenberg Uncertainty Principle**: Another neat feature in quantum mechanics is that you can't simultaneously measure non-commuting variables to an arbitrary precision. For example, the position and momentum of a particle cannot be both precisely measured at the same time.

Thus, measuring a quantum system has two profound implications: it changes the underlying system (known as the observer effect), and it gives only probabilistic results.

In terms of quantum circuits, the measurement process is usually indicated by a particular operation or gate in the end of the circuit that represents this process of observation or measurement. The output of a quantum circuit is then the set of measurements (or observed qubits) after the system collapses post these measurement operations.

These measurements are usually used in conjunction with other principles of quantum computing like interferences of the quantum states to create powerful computational algorithms which are much more efficient than classical counterparts in certain domains. But it's important to remember that due to the probabilistic nature of these measurements, quantum algorithms usually need to execute many times to obtain the correct output.

So, to summarize, measuring a quantum circuit means applying a measurement operation at the end of the computation (or at the points in the computation where measurements are required) and observing each quantum bit, which causes each to collapse to a traditional binary state (0 or 1). This process is inherently probabilistic, dependent on the coefficients specifying the state of the system, and fundamentally different than measurement in classical computing.

4.13   How does the no-cloning theorem impact the design of quantum circuits?

The no-cloning theorem states that it is impossible to create an identical copy of an arbitrary unknown quantum state. This is a fundamental principle of quantum mechanics and importantly differentiates quantum computing from classical computing, and it affects the design of quantum circuits in several ways:

1. **Designing Algorithms**: Quantum algorithms cannot rely on the ability to clone quantum states for redundancy or backup as in classical computing. This changes how algorithms are created, requiring a different approach that takes into account the no-cloning theorem.

2. **Error Correction**: In classical computers, error correction methods often rely on duplicating bits and checking their consistency. Due to the no-cloning theorem, similar error correction techniques are not directly applicable in quantum computing. Quantum error correction codes have to be specifically designed by taking this into account.

3. **Entanglement**: The impossibility of duplicating quantum states also contributes to the phenomenon of "quantum entanglement", where the state of coupled quantum systems cannot be described independently. Hence, quantum circuits need to be carefully designed to handle such phenomena.

4. **Information Transfer**: The no-cloning theorem implies that quantum information cannot be transmitted in the same way as classical information. This impacts not only the design of quantum circuits but also suggests exciting applications in secure information transfer like quantum cryptography.

5. **Measurement**: Quantum circuits need to be designed with the understanding that after a measure is performed on a qubit, its state collapses. We can't clone the state before measurement to study it further after measurement.

6. **Nondestructive Testing**: The no-cloning theorem precludes the possibility of nondestructive deterministic tests (in the sense of probing the complete information in the state of a quantum system).

It's also interesting to note that the proof of the no-cloning theorem hints at the form of quantum gates. Any unitary operator that can clone a state will fail to maintain the inner product between vectors (which represents the probability amplitude), and thus it won't be a valid quantum gate (as quantum gates must be unitary).

Therefore, it can be said that the no-cloning theorem plays a significant role in shaping the fundamental concepts and techniques of quantum circuits and quantum computing in general.

4.14   How does entanglement between qubits affect the operation of a quantum circuit?

Entanglement is a fundamental principle of quantum mechanics that allows quantum systems to exhibit correlations that are stronger than those achievable in classical systems. This quantum correlation plays a crucial role in many quantum information processing tasks such as quantum communication, quantum cryptography, and quantum computing.

Let's consider a quantum circuit with two qubits. Each qubit in a quantum circuit can exist in a superposition of states, meaning it can be in state $|0\rangle$, state $|1\rangle$, or any combination thereof. When two qubits become entangled, the state of one qubit becomes directly dependent on the state of the other, no matter how far apart they are.

This means that the information of one qubit cannot be completely described independently of the other.

In the context of quantum gates and circuits, this entanglement has profound implications:

* **Processing:** Quantum gates applied to one of the entangled qubits affect the entire system. For example, an application of a quantum gate on an entangled qubit may alter the state of its entangled partner instantaneously.

* **Information Transfer:** Entanglement can be utilized to transfer quantum information from one location to another, a process known as quantum teleportation.

* **Parallelism:** Entanglememt allows for the possibility of processing many combinations of bits simultaneously, a property which gives quantum computers their potential computational power.

* **Interference:** Entangled qubits can constructively and destructively interfere with each other, a feature that is exploited in several quantum algorithms, like Grover's or Shor's algorithm, to speed up the solution finding process.

Here is an example of a simple quantum circuit employing entanglement. Let's consider a two-qubit system with an initial state $|00\rangle$. The circuit applies a Hadamard gate (H) to the first qubit producing a superposition, followed by a controlled-NOT gate (CNOT) entangling the two qubits:

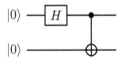

After the application of Hadamard gate, the state becomes $1/sqrt2(|0\rangle + |1\rangle) \otimes |0\rangle$, and after the CNOT gate, the state becomes $1/\sqrt{2}(|00\rangle + |11\rangle)$, which is an entangled state.

In this case, the measurement of the first qubit will instantaneously determine the state of the second one. If the first qubit is found to be in state $|0\rangle$, the second one will also be in state $|0\rangle$. If the first qubit is in state $|1\rangle$, the second one will be in state $|1\rangle$. This exemplifies the effects of entanglement in a quantum circuit.

4.15 How are quantum algorithms implemented using quantum circuits?

Quantum algorithms are implemented using quantum circuits by applying a sequence of quantum gates to qubits, the basic unit of quantum information. A quantum gate, like its classical analogue, performs operations on a small number of qubits. These gates are the building blocks of quantum circuits.

Here are some fundamental quantum gates: 1. Pauli X, Y and Z gates: These gates operate on a single qubit. The X gate is analogous to the classical NOT gate.

$$X = \begin{pmatrix} 0 & 1 \\ 1 & 0 \end{pmatrix}, Y = \begin{pmatrix} 0 & -i \\ i & 0 \end{pmatrix}, Z = \begin{pmatrix} 1 & 0 \\ 0 & -1 \end{pmatrix}$$

2. Hadamard Gate: This one-qubit gate creates superposition, a fundamental concept in quantum computing.

$$H = \frac{1}{\sqrt{2}} \begin{pmatrix} 1 & 1 \\ 1 & -1 \end{pmatrix}$$

3. Phase Gate: It applies a phase of a particular value to a qubit.

$$S = \begin{pmatrix} 1 & 0 \\ 0 & i \end{pmatrix}$$

4. Controlled operation gates: These operate on 2 or more qubits where the state of one qubit determines the operation on another

qubit. The most famous of these is the CNOT (Controlled-NOT) gate.

$$\text{CNOT} = \begin{pmatrix} 1 & 0 & 0 & 0 \\ 0 & 1 & 0 & 0 \\ 0 & 0 & 0 & 1 \\ 0 & 0 & 1 & 0 \end{pmatrix}$$

To compose a quantum algorithm, one combines these gates into a quantum circuit. As a basic example, suppose we want to prepare a Bell State. This is achieved using Hadamard gate and CNOT gate:

1. Apply a Hadamard gate on the first qubit to generate superposition.

2. Apply a CNOT gate with the first qubit as control and the second qubit as target.

This puts the qubits into an entangled state, which is used in numerous quantum algorithms.

The manipulation of these gates in the quantum circuit is what enables complex computation in quantum computing. By carefully manipulating qubit states and applying the correct sequence of gates, a variety of algorithms can be implemented, such as Shor's Algorithm for factoring and Grover's Algorithm for search.

Chapter 5

Quantum Algorithms

In this chapter, we dive into the fascinating domain of quantum algorithms. We explore popular algorithms like Grover's and Shor's, and delve into the burgeoning field of quantum machine learning algorithms, revealing how quantum principles can potentially provide exponential computational speed-ups.

5.1 How do quantum algorithms differ from classical ones?

The key difference between quantum algorithms and classical algorithms lies in the nature of computation and information processing.

Classical algorithms operate on classical bits, where each bit is either in a state of 0 or 1 at any given point in time. However, quantum algorithms operate on quantum bits (qubits), where a qubit can be in a state of 0, 1, or both due to the property of superposition.

This ability to hold multiple states simultaneously allows quantum

algorithms to process a large number of possibilities at once, which
can lead to superior performance for certain types of problems. These
issues include factoring large numbers, simulating quantum systems,
performing certain database searches, and solving specific optimization problems.

Furthermore, quantum algorithms also exploit another quantum feature known as entanglement, where the state of one qubit becomes
correlated with the state of another. This can lead to intricate quantum states and correlations that can be used to process information
in ways that would be impossible classically.

Mathematically, a classical algorithm might process information in a
linear data flow, where each step is a logical operation (e.g., AND,
OR, NOT). Here's an example in pseudo-code that reverses an array:

```
for i in 0 to n/2:
    temp = array[i]
    array[i] = array[n-i-1]
    array[n-i-1] = temp
```

However, a quantum algorithm processes information in a superimposed data flow, using operations (called quantum gates) that manipulate multiple states simultaneously. Here's a simple example of
a quantum algorithm, the Deustch's algorithm, in quantum circuit
notation:

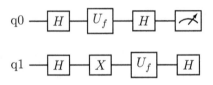

Where 'H' is the Hadamard gate, 'Uf' is the quantum oracle, 'X' is
the bit-flip gate, 'M' denotes measurement.

These differences make quantum algorithms potentially more powerful than classical ones for certain tasks. However, their practical real-

ization requires the construction and operation of large-scale quantum computers, which is still an active area of research.

5.2 Can you provide examples of problems that quantum algorithms can solve more efficiently than classical ones?

Two quintessential examples are Shor's algorithm and Grover's algorithm.

Shor's algorithm is known for factoring large numbers into primes efficiently. A classical computer needs to perform this task in time that grows exponentially with the size of the input while Shor's algorithm can do it in polynomial time. This represents a significant speed up compared with classical factoring algorithms.

Mathematically;

The best classical factoring algorithm runs in time $\exp(O((logN)^(1/3)*(loglogN)^(2/3)))$ while Shor's quantum algorithm runs in time $O((logN)^2(loglogN)(logloglogN))$ which is polynomially fast.

Grover's algorithm on the other hand provides quadratic speedup for unsorted database search. Classical algorithm takes linear time, O(N), while Grover's algorithm can do it in time $\sqrt{N}$.

Let's consider searching for a number in an unsorted database of N elements.

Classical computer on average needs to look at half the elements, so time complexity would be 0.5N. Quantum computer using Grover's algorithm finds the element in $\sqrt{N}$ operations.

These are not the only algorithms quantum computing is capable of speeding up. There are many other quantum algorithms such as quantum phase estimation, quantum counting, quantum amplitude estimation and more that are designed to solve specific computational problems more efficiently than classical algorithms.

However, it's important to note that quantum computers and algorithms are not necessarily faster or more efficient for all classes of problems. In fact, there are many problems where classical computers are currently faster and more efficient due to technological constraints and error rates of current quantum computers. Quantum advantage truly shines in a specific subset of problems.

5.3   What does quantum speedup mean, and how does it relate to quantum algorithms?

Quantum speedup refers to the potential advantage that quantum algorithms offer over the classical algorithms in solving certain types of problems. This advantage can be attributed to a phenomenon known as quantum parallelism, which allows quantum systems to perform many calculations simultaneously — not to be confused with parallelism in classical computing, which also performs many operations simultaneously but on different processors.

Quantum speedup is often categorized into two types: polynomial speedup and exponential speedup. Polynomial speedup refers to the scenario where a problem that requires classical computation time n^k can be solved in quantum computation time n^b, where b<k. Exponential speedup is more notable, referring to situations where a problem that would require exponential time on classical computers can be solved in polynomial time on a quantum computer. An example of exponential speedup is Shor's algorithm for integer factorization, which has significant implications for cryptography.

More formally, let's use the time complexity notation for algorithms. If T(n) is the time complexity of a classical algorithm for a problem of size n, and Q(n) is the time complexity of a quantum algorithm for the same problem, then the quantum speedup S(n) is given by:

$$S(n) = T(n)/Q(n)$$

The larger S(n) is, the greater the speedup. If S(n) is exponential, then the quantum algorithm is exponentially faster than the best known or possible classical algorithm.

Note that quantum speedup is a theoretical concept; whether or not a quantum speedup can be achieved in practice depends on various factors, such as the ability to build and maintain a large-scale quantum computer, the difficulty of implementing the quantum algorithm, and the required coherence time of the quantum computer. As such, while the potential power of quantum algorithms is immense, realizing this potential is a significant challenge in the field of quantum computing.

5.4   How are quantum algorithms executed on a quantum computer?

Quantum algorithms are executed on a quantum computer using a two-step process: building a quantum circuit and executing a quantum measurement.

1. **Building a Quantum Circuit:**

The first step involves constructing a quantum circuit, which is basically the quantum version of a flowchart. We build a quantum circuit using quantum gates. These gates manipulate qubits - the basic units of quantum information, analogous to classical bits. Unlike classical bits, however, a qubit can be in a state that is a superposition of both 0 and 1 simultaneously, allowing quantum computation to explore a much larger space of states.

A quantum circuit is made up of several quantum gates applied in a specific order. This order, and the choice of gates, is determined by the specific quantum algorithm being executed.

2. **Executing a Quantum Measurement:**

Once we have a quantum circuit, the next step is to process it on a quantum computer. This involves preparing an initial state of qubits (usually all set to 0), applying the quantum gates, and then measuring the final state of the qubits.

Measurement in the quantum world is different from classical measurement. When we measure a qubit, the superposition collapses to either 0 or 1, and we get that as our output. Moreover, each measurement can give different results because quantum measurements are inherently probabilistic.

So, quantum computing involves manipulating qubits with quantum gates and then making a probabilistic measurement. The success of the computation often depends on the likelihood of getting the correct answer from this probabilistic distribution - the higher the probability, the fewer times we need to repeat the computation.

Here is a brief example of what each part of a quantum algorithm looks like, using the Deustch-Josza algorithm as an example. It's a simple algorithm used for solving the Deutsch-Josza problem with a single query to the oracle, using the principle of quantum superposition and interference.

The Deutsch-Josza Algorithm:

1. Prepare two quantum registers. The first is an n-qubit register initialized to |0>, and the second is a one-qubit register initialized to |1>:

$$|\psi_1\rangle = |0...0\rangle|1\rangle$$

2. Apply the Hadamard gate to each qubit:

$$|\psi_2\rangle = (H^{\otimes}n \otimes H)|\psi_1\rangle = \frac{1}{\sqrt{2^n}} \sum_{x=0}^{2^n-1} |x\rangle(|0\rangle - |1\rangle)$$

3. Apply the quantum oracle Uf:

$$|\psi_3\rangle = Uf|\psi_2\rangle = \frac{1}{\sqrt{2^n}} \sum_{x=0}^{2^n-1} |x\rangle|f(x)\rangle$$

4. Apply the Hadamard gate to the first n qubits again:

$$|\psi_4\rangle = (H^{\otimes n} \otimes I)|\psi_3\rangle = \frac{1}{2^{n/2}} \sum_{x=0}^{2^n-1} (-1)^{f(x)}|x\rangle|f(x)\rangle$$

5. Then measure the first register.

The job of the quantum oracle is to apply a phase flip to the amplitude of the state $|x\rangle$ in the superposition if and only if f(x) = 1.

Measurement post-selects the elements with $f(x) = 0$ with nonzero amplitude and hence distinguishes between a constant and a balanced function. This is achieved with only one call to the function f, unlike classical deterministic computations which require $2^{n-1} + 1$ calls in the worst-case scenario.

Thus, quantum computation allows us to solve certain problems more efficiently than classical computation.

5.5   What role do superposition and entanglement play in quantum algorithms?

Superposition and entanglement are the core principles that quantum algorithms leverage to solve problems more efficiently than classical algorithms.

1. **Superposition**

Superposition refers to the ability of quantum systems to exist in multiple states at once. While classical bits can only exist in one of two states (0 or 1), a quantum bit or "qubit" can exist in a superposition of states. This means a qubit can simultaneously be in a state $|0>$ and $|1>$. Specifically, it could be in a state:

$$|\psi\rangle = \alpha|0\rangle + \beta|1\rangle$$

where α and β are complex coefficients and $|\alpha|^2 + |\beta|^2 = 1$.

This property leads to an exponential increase in the computational space. If you have 'n' qubits in superposition, you can represent 2^n different states. For example, two classical bits can represent one of four states (00, 01, 10, 11), while two qubits in superposition can represent all four states at once.

2. **Entanglement**

Entanglement is a uniquely quantum mechanical phenomenon where two or more particles become interlinked and the state of one particle is directly related to the state of the other, no matter how far they are separated. In a system of two entangled qubits, the state of the system can be described as:

$$|\psi\rangle = \alpha|00\rangle + \beta|11\rangle$$

Where α and β are complex coefficients and $|\alpha|^2 + |\beta|^2 = 1$.

Such a state can't be factored into two separate qubit states, which suggests a deep connection between the qubits. This allows quantum algorithms to solve problems by manipulating an entangled group of qubits all at once, thus improving computational speed and efficiency.

Quantum algorithms, such as Shor's algorithm for factorizing large numbers or Grover's algorithm for unordered database searches, heavily rely on superposition for parallelism and entanglement for correlation and manipulation of qubits.

For example, in Grover's algorithm, superposition is used to initialize the search space, and quantum entanglement and interference are then used to mark and amplify the unique solution out of all possibilities, which leads to a quadratically faster search compared to classical search algorithms.

The strength of quantum algorithms lies in extracting information from this quantum states space containing superposition and entanglement without collapsing it back to classical bits. Therefore, the art of developing quantum algorithms often involves designing procedures that interfere different computational paths in such a way that desired solutions reinforce while undesired solutions cancel out, which often rely on the principles of superposition and entanglement.

5.6 What is Grover's algorithm, and what types of problems does it address?

Grover's algorithm, proposed by Lov Grover in 1996, is a quantum algorithm that is significant in searching unstructured databases with an $N = 2^n$ number of items, where n is the number of qubits in the system, approximately quadratically faster than its classical counterparts.

In more technical terms, Grover's algorithm is used to find the unique input to a black-box function that produces a particular output value, using just $O(\sqrt{N})$ evaluations of the function, where N is the size of the function's domain.

The type of problem that Grover's algorithm addresses is known as **unstructured search problem** or **Oracle problem**. Such problem consists in finding a particular element in an unstructured list by querying about elements. Unstructured means that there are no specific patterns in the location or value of the items, and we have no prior knowledge about where it is, so the only option is to search the whole list.

For instance, classic unstructured search would require on average

$N/2$ and in worst case N queries to find the desired element. Yet Grover's algorithm outperforms classical search by solving such problem in approximately $\sqrt{N}$ quantum operations which indicates a quadratic speedup over classic search.

Here is a brief walkthrough of the algorithm:

1. Initialize a register of n qubits to the state $|0^n>$

$$|0^n\rangle = |0\rangle \otimes |0\rangle \otimes ... \otimes |0\rangle = \begin{bmatrix} 1 \\ 0 \\ \vdots \\ 0 \end{bmatrix}$$

2. Create an equal superposition state of all computational basis states (we call this stage Amplitude Amplification) using Hadamard Transform.

$$H^{\otimes n}|0^n\rangle = \frac{1}{\sqrt{N}} \sum_{x=0}^{N-1} |x\rangle$$

3. For approximately $\sqrt{N}$ times, repeat:

- Apply the black-box function U_f which flips the sign of the state's phase wherever the function $f(x)$ is 1.

- Apply the Grover diffusion operator which inverses the amplitude around the average amplitude.

One caution about Grover's algorithm is the number of iterations. If we iterate further than optimal $\sqrt{N}$ number of times, the success probability will decrease.

In conclusion, Grover's algorithm shows the potential of quantum computing to massively increase processing speed, not only for searching databases but also for a myriad of other applications that require search operations.

5.7 How does Grover's algorithm leverage quantum mechanics to improve search efficiency?

Grover's algorithm is a quantum algorithm that finds with high probability the unique input to a black box function that produces a particular output value, using just $O(\sqrt{N})$ evaluations of the function, where N is the size of the function's domain. This is a quadratic improvement over the best possible classical algorithm, which would need to evaluate the function $O(N)$ times in the worst-case scenario.

Here is how it works:

The central quantum trick in Grover's algorithm is the use of interference of amplitudes, typical to quantum mechanics.

1. **Initialization**

Start with an N state quantum system in a superposition of all possible states.

$$|\psi\rangle = \frac{1}{\sqrt{N}} \sum_{x=0}^{N-1} |x\rangle$$

2. **Oracle Application**

Grover's algorithm uses an oracle to mark the sought-after states. Being in the state $|x\rangle$, the oracle changes the phase of the system, depending on whether x is in the sought-after states.

A transformation U_ω is applied to the state which flips the sign of the marked item.

$$U_\omega|\psi\rangle = \frac{1}{\sqrt{N}} \sum_{x=0}^{N-1} y_x|x\rangle$$

Here, $y_x = -1$ if x is the marked item and 1 otherwise.

3. **Diffusion Operator**

After applying the oracle, another transformation known as the Grover diffusion operator or Grover iterate, denoted U_s, is applied. This operation performs an inversion about the average amplitude.

$$U_s = 2|s\rangle\langle s| - I$$

Here, $|s\rangle = \frac{1}{\sqrt{N}} \sum_{x=0}^{N-1} |x\rangle$ is the equal superposition state and I is the identity operator.

Subsequent applications of U_ω and U_s will increase the amplitude of the marked item(s) while decreasing the amplitude of the unmarked items.

4. **Iterate**

Repeat the application of U_ω and U_s about $\sqrt{N}$ times to maximize the probability of measuring the marked item.

This process constructs and then manipulates a quantum superposition of all 2^N candidate solutions, effectively carrying out a parallel search of the search space. Omega is the unknown solution to the black-box problem, and the Grover iteration is designed to rotate the initial state towards this solution.

In terms of complexity analysis, classical deterministic search algorithms have a linear query complexity of $O(N)$, whereas Grover's quantum search algorithm improves this to $O(\sqrt{N})$, a profound leap. Even its fundamental lower bound makes it faster than any classical algorithm. Thus, Grover's algorithm is optimal, providing a quantum speedup against the best possible classical search algorithms.

5.8 Can you walk through the process of Grover's algorithm with an example?

Grover's Algorithm is a quantum algorithm for searching an unsorted database with quadratic speedup. It provides a good example of quantum speedup, with its $\sqrt{N}$ complexity compared to a classical search's linear $O(N)$ complexity.

Let's assume we have 4 elements in our database, making our search space 2^2 possibilities (hence, we'll use 2 qubits).

These are indexed as $|00>$, $|01>$, $|10>$, and $|11>$.

Let's say '11' is the target.

Grover's Algorithm follows these steps:

1. **Initialization**: Set up a uniform superposition of all possible states. This is achieved by applying Hadamard gates to all qubits, which are initially in the state $|0>$.

So,
$$|\psi\rangle = H|x\rangle = 1/2(|00\rangle + |01\rangle + |10\rangle + |11\rangle)$$

2. **Oracle Application**: Apply the quantum oracle (aka black box). This oracle flips the sign of the state that corresponds to the solution. Here, $|11>$ is our solution, so the state becomes:

$$|\psi'\rangle = 1/2(|00\rangle + |01\rangle + |10\rangle - |11\rangle)$$

3. **Diffusion Operator**: Apply the Grover diffusion operator. It flips about the mean amplitude.

- First, apply a Hadamard gate to all qubits, giving

$$|\psi''\rangle = H|\psi'\rangle = 1/2(|0\rangle - |1\rangle - |2\rangle + |3\rangle) = 1/2(|00\rangle - |01\rangle - |10\rangle + |11\rangle)$$

- Then, apply the operation $2|0><0| - I$, which gives

$$|\psi'''\rangle = (2|0><0| - I)|\psi''\rangle = 1/2(-|00\rangle + |01\rangle + |10\rangle - |11\rangle)$$

- Finally, apply the Hadamard gate to all qubits again. This could be understood as reflection through the average amplitude.

After all these steps, you will find that your quantum state is now closer to $|11\rangle$ than before.

4. **Iterate**: Repeat the oracle and diffusion operator, but remember, there is a limitation based on the principle of optimal stopping. The optimal number of iterations is '$\sqrt{N}$'. After these iterations, we can perform a measurement, and the probability of obtaining $|11>$ would be the highest.

For larger search spaces, Grover's Algorithm is particularly powerful when compared to classical search algorithms, as the quantum algorithm scales favourably in comparison due to the property of quantum superposition.

Remember Grover's Algorithm doesn't give you the exact solution after iteration, instead, it improves the probability of hitting the right answer. Once you exceed the optimal number of iterations, the performance starts to degrade. A part of the algorithm's process is to find this "sweet spot" of maximum probability for the right answer.

Hopefully, this clarifies the process of Grover's Algorithm. Keep in mind we used only a 2-bit example, while in practice, quantum computers operate with a significantly larger number of bits.

5.9   What is the speedup provided by Grover's algorithm compared to classical algorithms?

Grover's algorithm offers a quadratic speedup over the classical computation.

To make this clearer, let's look at it in detail.

In a classical computing scenario, in order to find a specific item in an unsorted database of N items, in the worst-case scenario, one would have to look at each item in sequence. Therefore, you'd need to look at N items in total. In other words, the search problem complexity is O(N) in classical computational terms.

On the other hand, Grover's algorithm reduces this complexity dramatically. The quantum algorithm can find the required item in approximately √N iterations. Therefore, we say that Grover's algorithm has a time complexity of O(√N).

This makes Grover's algorithm significantly superior to classical ones for unstructured search problem, providing a quadratic speedup. It's important to note that while this speedup is significant, it does not offer the exponential speedup that some quantum algorithms give for such problems as factoring large numbers.

In mathematical terms, the comparison can be illustrated by the following:

$$\text{Classical Algorithm Time Complexity} : O(N)$$

$$\text{Grover's Algorithm Time Complexity} : O\left(\sqrt{N}\right)$$

Keep in mind that it works best when the solution is unique. As more solutions are added, the speedup provided reduces and eventually converges to a classical algorithm's speed.

5.10   Are there any limitations or downsides to using Grover's algorithm?

Grover's algorithm is known for its ability to conduct unstructured data search tasks in a faster and more efficient manner than classical search algorithms. However, despite its numerous advantages, there are some limitations and downsides linked to Grover's algorithm which include:

1. **Data preparation**: Preparing the necessary quantum state in which the quantum search will operate can be really complex. The database to be searched has to be encoded into the amplitude of the quantum states which can be computationally challenging and time-consuming, especially for larger databases.

2. **Error correction**: Quantum computers are extremely sensitive to errors due to decoherence. This places a limitation on the real-world use of Grover's algorithm, as current quantum computers frequently encounter errors. Error correction schemes could be applied to fix such issues, but they often require additional qubits, making the process more complex and less efficient.

3. **No speedup for NP-complete problems**: It is sometimes mistakenly assumed that Grover's algorithm could be used to provide a super-polynomial speedup for NP-complete problems, as it does for search problems. However, this is not the case because the great speedup only applies to decision problems, not optimization problems.

4. **Oracles**: Grover's algorithm requires the use of a "quantum oracle" to mark the desired elements in the search space. Designing this oracle can be non-trivial and may not always be possible.

5. **Quantum resources**: Grover's algorithm, like all quantum algorithms, requires a fault-tolerant quantum computer to run. Currently, this technology is in its infancy and therefore imposes a practical limitation to using Grover's algorithm.

Yet it's worth mentioning that despite these limitations, Grover's algorithm provides a significant quadratic improvement in search problems over classical algorithms, and has strategic value in the fields of database search, cryptography, etc. The development of practical quantum computing technology can largely mitigate these downsides.

5.11 What is Shor's algorithm and why is it significant?

Shor's algorithm, proposed by Peter Shor in 1994, is a quantum algorithm for factoring large numbers into their prime factors in polynomial time, a stark contrast to the best known classical algorithms which solve the problem in exponential time. This is substantial because the difficulty of factoring large numbers is the basis for most public key cryptography systems, including the RSA algorithm.

The algorithm also estimates the period of a modular function. Shor's algorithm employs the quantum Fourier transform, in particular, entanglement and interference, to greatly increase factoring speed.

Mathematically, Shor's algorithm involves three primary steps:

1. Initialize two quantum registers (sets of qubits) and entangle them.

2. Apply a quantum version of the modular exponentiation function, which entangles the two registers.

3. Apply a Quantum Fourier Transform (QFT) to one of the registers, which amplifies the desired states.

To illustrate, consider that we want to factor a large composite number N. The algorithm begins by guessing a random number a less than N, and checking to see whether a and N have any common factors (using Euclid's algorithm). If they do, then we have found a nontrivial factor of N. If they do not, then we proceed to the quantum phase of the algorithm.

Shor's algorithm is monumental in the field of quantum computing because it provides a clear example of a problem for which quantum computers (if they can be built) will be exponentially faster than classical computers. This speed-up could potentially make RSA encryption, which is commonly used in secure data transmission, vulnerable, thus prompting the study of post-quantum cryptography schemes.

For a practical example, consider trying to factor 15. Using Shor's algorithm, you would find the period of the function $f(x) = 11^x$ mod 15. After preparing an equal superposition of all inputs and their corresponding outputs in the two quantum registers, and applying a QFT, you would measure the second register to find that the period is 4. Thus $a^{r/2} \pm 1$ (11 to the power of half the period plus or minus 1) gives you factors of 15, namely 5 and 3.

5.12 How does Shor's algorithm exploit quantum computing to factor large numbers efficiently?

Shor's algorithm is a quantum algorithm, that when implemented on a quantum computer, can factor large numbers exponentially faster than the best known classical factoring algorithm. It's the most famous quantum algorithm due to its potential implications on cryptography, given that the security of many cryptographic systems relies on the difficulty of factoring large numbers.

The algorithm takes advantage of superposition, interference, and entanglement - the fundamental principles of quantum physics that a quantum computer can naturally exploit.

Here's a simplified, step-by-step explanation of how it works:

1. **Superposition** : The quantum computer is set up in a superposition of states, each representing a possible solution (i.e., a possible factor of the number to be factored). In more precise terms, given an integer N that we wish to factor, a superposition of states from 0 to $N - 1$ is created.

2. **Application of the Quantum Oracle (Modular Exponentiation Function)** : Each state is then transformed using a quantum oracle or a function that encodes the problem to be solved. For Shor's algorithm, this oracle is a modular exponentiation function, effectively

computing a^x mod N for a being a coprime of N and all x in the superposition. This results in an entangled state, where each input value x is mapped to a result a^x mod N.

3. **Quantum Fourier transform** : The quantum Fourier transform (QFT) is applied, a linear transformation that maps each state to a new state where the probability of observing any given state reflects the periodicity of the function applied. This converts the periodicity of the above function from the previous step into a form where it can be recognized or measured via phase estimation.

4. **Measurement and Classical Post-processing** : The state of the quantum computer is measured, collapsing the superposition and providing a value that, after some classical post-processing (i.e., classical computation), yields the factors of the number. The classical post-processing usually involves using Euclid's algorithm for computing the greatest common divisor (GCD).

While quantum computers capable of running Shor's algorithm on large numbers do not yet exist, Shor's algorithm is proof that quantum computers could, in theory, solve certain problems much faster than classical computers. This potential is an important motivation for ongoing research and development in quantum computing.

5.13   What implications does Shor's algorithm have for current cryptographic methods?

Shor's algorithm has profound implications for current cryptographic methods, especially for the widely used RSA (Rivest-Shamir-Adleman) cryptosystem.

The RSA encryption method heavily relies on the fact that classical computers take a long time (exponential time) to factor large numbers into primes, a process which is critical for breaking the RSA encryption. While it's relatively easy to multiply two prime numbers together to form a larger number, finding the prime factors of a large number is effectively impossible using classical algorithms when the numbers get large enough. This is referred to as a "trap-door" function: easy in one direction, difficult in the other.

However, Shor's quantum algorithm can theoretically factor large numbers in polynomial time, meaning an efficient implementation of Shor's algorithm could break RSA encryption. Here's the difference in scaling:

1. Classical factorization grows exponentially with the size of the input (bit-length 'n'). The best known algorithm is the general number field sieve with time complexity roughly $\exp((64/9 * (ln(n))^{1/3} * (ln(ln(n)))^{2/3}))$.

2. Shor's algorithm scales polynomially with 'n', specifically as $O((n^2)* (log(n)) * (log(log(n))))$.

This time complexity difference implies that a sufficiently large quantum computer running Shor's algorithm could factor large numbers much more efficiently than classical computers, thus breaking the security of cryptosystems like RSA.

However, it's important to emphasize that as of now, quantum computers capable of running Shor's algorithm at a scale to threaten current cryptographic systems do not yet exist. The largest number to date to be factored by a quantum computer using Shor's algorithm is 21, which was accomplished with much effort. Scaling up the process is a current area of intensive research in quantum computing.

Looking forward, understanding the implications of Shor's algorithm is critical for the development of post-quantum cryptography, which involves creating cryptographic systems that are secure even against quantum computers. For example, lattice-based encryption and hash-based cryptography are considered to be promising directions for post-quantum cryptography, as they rely on mathematical problems that are believed to be hard for both classical and quantum computers.

5.14   Can you explain how Shor's algorithm works with an example?

Shor's algorithm is a quantum algorithm that finds the prime factors of a given number, N. It does this in polynomial time (as opposed to classical algorithms, which do this in exponential time), making it an example of quantum supremacy.

Shor's algorithm consists of two parts:

1. A quantum period-finding subroutine which, given $a < m$ and the ability to compute $f(x) = a^x \bmod m$ on a quantum computer, finds the period r of $f(x)$.

2. A classical polynomial-time algorithm that finds the greatest common divisor of numbers.

###Explanation of Shor's algorithm:

1. Choose a random number $a < N$.

2. Compute the greatest common divisor of a and N using the Euclidean method.

 - If $\text{GCD}(a, N) \neq 1$, this implies that a is a nontrivial factor of N.

 - If $\text{GCD}(a, N) = 1$, we proceed to the quantum part of the algorithm.

3. Find the period t of the function $f(x) = a^x \bmod N$ using the quantum subroutine.

4. If t is odd or if $a^{t/2}$ is equivalent to $-1 \bmod N$, return to step 1.

5. Otherwise, the greatest common divisor of N and both $a^{t/2} \pm 1$ will give nontrivial factors of N.

Let's take an example:

###Example:

Let $N = 15$, factorization of which is to be found.

1. Select a random number $a < N$. Let's choose $a = 7$.

2. The GCD of $(7, 15)$ is 1 and hence, we proceed to the quantum part.

3. Let's assume that the quantum part of the algorithm gives us the period $t = 2$ for the function $f(x) = 7^x \bmod 15$.

4. t is even and $7^{t/2} = 7 \bmod 15$ is not -1, so proceed further.

5. Now, compute $\mathrm{GCD}(N, 7^1 + 1) = \mathrm{GCD}(15, 8) = 1$ and $\mathrm{GCD}(N, 7^1 - 1)$ $= \mathrm{GCD}(15, 6) = 3$

6. So, we repeat the entire process.

This may continue until we find all factors. In this case, the final factors are indeed 3 and 5.

Shor's algorithm shows how quantum computers can solve certain problems faster than classical computers and it is one of the main reasons for the interest in building quantum computers.

5.15   What are the challenges of implementing Shor's algorithm on a real-world quantum computer?

Shor's algorithm is a quantum algorithm that solves the problem of integer factorization exponentially faster than the best-known classical algorithms. However, its practical implementation on real-world quantum computers presents several significant challenges:

1. **Number of qubits:** The execution of Shor's algorithm requires a significant number of qubits. For instance, factoring a 2048-bit RSA integer would require around 4096 qubits. Current quantum hardware has not yet reached the scale to support such a number of qubits.

2. **Quantum error correction:** Quantum computers are highly

sensitive to errors, which are inevitable in practice due to reasons like noise and loss of quantum coherence (also known as decoherence). To effectively implement Shor's algorithm, we need to apply Quantum Error Correction (QEC) techniques. The necessity of QEC further escalates the requirement of the number of qubits, making it even more challenging with the current quantum hardware.

3. **Circuit depth issue:** The quantum circuit that describes Shor's algorithm is deep and involves many layers of logic gates. With today's noisy intermediate-scale quantum (NISQ) computers, the error rates are often too high to execute deep circuits of this kind successfully.

4. **Measurement Precision:** High precision is required to obtain the result of Shor's algorithm. Since Shor's algorithm uses a Quantum Fourier Transform (QFT), the accuracy of the result can be affected by the precision of the measurements, which is challenging to achieve.

In a nutshell, to implement Shor's algorithm on a real-world quantum computer, the primary requirements are a large, error-corrected, and highly precise quantum computer. Current quantum technology has not yet reached this level of maturity.

To visualize this, an example of Shor's algorithm implementation circuit for input 15 is shown below:

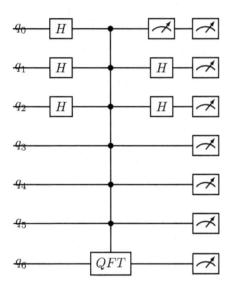

This circuit includes multiple quantum gates which compound to present a highly complex and deep algorithm. The measurement result helps to extract the phase which corresponds to the periodicity of the function, an essential step to finding the factors of a composite number.

Chapter 6

Quantum Error Correction

Chapter six addresses a crucial aspect of quantum computing—error correction. We explore the origins of quantum noise and decoherence, discuss various error correction codes, and understand the concept of fault tolerance, all crucial for the practical realization of robust quantum computers.

6.1 What is quantum noise, and how does it impact quantum computations?

Quantum noise refers to any extrinsic factors that contribute to uncertainties or errors in a quantum system's state. It can be a result of environmental fluctuations affecting quantum bits (qubits), imperfect gate operations, or faulty measurements. Because quantum systems are extremely sensitive to disturbances, such noise can greatly impact the information stored in qubits and the fidelity of quantum computations.

The unique feature of quantum computations - namely, quantum superposition and entanglement - allows quantum computers to perform complex computations exponentially faster than classical computers. However, these quantum properties are fragile and can be easily destroyed by environmental noise or imperfect operations, a phenomenon known as "decoherence", which hampers the reliability of quantum computations. As an example, if we are processing on a qubit in a superposition state $\frac{1}{\sqrt{2}}(|0\rangle + |1\rangle)$, any slight disturbance could collapse it to either $|0\rangle$ or $|1\rangle$.

Quantum error correction (QEC) is one of the principal methods used to preserve quantum information from the deleterious effects of quantum noise. Unlike classical error correction that deals with bit flips (0 to 1, or 1 to 0), quantum error correction has to account for more complex errors due to the quantum nature of qubits. QEC methods aim to detect and correct errors without disturbing the overall state of the quantum system, a task that is achieved through redundancy and specialized quantum gates to ensure that calculations remain accurate.

6.2   How does quantum decoherence pose a challenge to the development of quantum computers?

Quantum decoherence poses a significant challenge to the development of quantum computers. Decoherence is essentially the process through which a quantum system loses its quantum properties, and interacts with its environment in such a way that it gradually loses its ability to maintain superposition and entanglement, the essential elements of quantum computing.

In classical computing, bits have well-defined states – either 0 or 1. However, in quantum computing, qubits (quantum bits) can exist in a superposition of states. When qubits interact with their environment, their quantum state can partially collapse due to the process of decoherence. As a result, the qubits' superposition is lost, along with any quantum computation that was underway.

Let me show this with a simple conceptual model. Consider a single qubit, which in the ideal case evolves according to its Hamiltonian H. Its state at time t is $|\psi(t)\rangle = e^{-iHt}|\psi(0)\rangle$.

Now let's introduce an environment (bath) B, with a Hamiltonian H_B and a total system Hamiltonian $H_T = H + H_B + H_{int}$, where H_{int} is the interaction Hamiltonian. At time $t = 0$, the state of the whole system might be $|\Psi(0)\rangle = |\psi(0)\rangle|B(0)\rangle$ where $|B(0)\rangle$ is the initial state of the bath. As time progresses, this state evolves according to the full Hamiltonian:

$$|\Psi(t)\rangle = e^{-iH_T t}|\Psi(0)\rangle$$

As a result, the state of the qubit becomes entangled with the state of the bath. This causes a loss of quantum information from the qubit to the bath, undermining the coherence of the quantum system and hence the computational potential.

In real life application of quantum computing, we aim to counter this loss of information through quantum error correction mechanisms, which are able to detect and correct for quantum errors without collapsing the superposition state of the quantum computer. These involve constructing quantum error-correcting codes, which operate through the creation of entangled states that can detect when qubits have been flipped due to interaction with the environment. However, designing systems that can effectively implement these codes is a non-trivial challenge and is a current area of ongoing research in the field.

6.3   What strategies are employed to minimize the effects of decoherence in a quantum system?

There are a number of strategies used to correct for the errors in a quantum system that are caused by factors such as decoherence. Here are some of the most common ones:

1. **Quantum Error Correction Codes:** This is the most prevalent strategy used to correct for quantum errors. These codes work by encoding a single quantum bit (qubit) of information across multiple physical qubits. If an error occurs in one of the physical qubits, it can be detected and corrected by measuring the state of the other qubits. There are several types of quantum error correction codes, including the Shor code, Steane code, and surface codes, each having their unique strengths and weaknesses.

2. **Decoherence-Free Subspaces (DFSs):** With DFSs, we use the symmetry properties of the quantum system and the environment it interacts with. By using these properties, we can find a subspace in which the quantum state can evolve without experiencing decoherence. DFSs are particularly useful for handling collective errors (those impacting multiple qubits simultaneously).

3. **Dynamical Decoupling (DD):** Somewhat similar to "spinning" a classical top to prevent it from falling over, dynamical decoupling applies a series of fast, periodic pulse operations to the system. Effectively, this aims to 'average out' the effect of the system's interaction with the external environment, therefore reducing the amount of decoherence experienced.

4. **Quantum Error Avoidance:** This method involves carefully designing the system and under particular constraints to prevent the occurrence of errors, rather than correcting them after they occur. For instance, we might work with qubits that are very well isolated from their environment.

5. **Topological Quantum Error Correction:** It's a sophisticated method that uses properties of topological phases of matter to correct errors. The benefit of this strategy is that it's robust against any type of local error as long as it doesn't impact too many qubits at once. This is due to the global, non-local nature of topological order.

Here's a table that shows the general methods mentioned along with their advantages and disadvantages:

Method	Advantage	Disadvantage
Quantum Error Correction Codes	Effective in a variety of environments	Requires extra resources (Additional qubits)
Decoherence-Free Subspaces	Avoids rather than corrects errors	Only works under certain conditions
Dynamical Decoupling	Simple and does not require extra qubits	Not always effective
Quantum Error Avoidance	Can prevent errors from occurring	Difficult to achieve in practice
Topological Quantum Error Correction	Highly robust	Technically challenging, requiring sophisticated manipulation and control over qubits

Table 6.1: Advantages and Disadvantages of Quantum Error Correction Methods

The right approach will depend on many factors such as the specific quantum system one is working with and the nature of the decoherence it experiences, the resources available, and so on.

6.4   How does quantum error correction help combat quantum noise and decoherence?

Quantum error correction (QEC) plays a crucial role in robust quantum computation by protecting quantum information from errors due to quantum "noise" and decoherence. The noise can result in unwanted changes to the state of qubits, while decoherence can lead to losses of quantum information before computations can be concluded.

In classical computing, error correction employs redundancy to form checks and balances on information. It uses additional bits to encode the information so that it's possible to detect and correct errors. The process modulates information into an error-correcting code and decodes it for computation.

However, Quantum Computing needs a distinct approach because direct replicas of quantum states are not possible due to the no-cloning theorem. Moreover, measuring the quantum state for error correction would likely collapse it because of the quantum measurement postulate.

To overcome these difficulties, QEC employs quantum entanglement and interference. Quantum states are encoded in such a way that if an error occurs, it creates an observable change in the quantum state that can be detected without measuring the encoded state itself. Quantum gates are utilized to perform error correction operations to return the system to its intended state.

In terms of combatting quantum noise and decoherence:

1. Quantum Noise: QEC manages quantum noise by identifying its impact on the state of qubits and by making the necessary corrections. At the basic level, QEC employs quantum parity checks that can detect bit-flip and phase-flip errors which are common in quantum computing.

2. Decoherence: Decoherence poses a significant challenge on preserving quantum coherence over time - a key requirement for quantum computation. Essentially, decoherence affects the superposed states of qubits, forcing them to lose their quantum mechanical properties and behave like classical bits. QEC addresses this problem by pinpointing the errors and performing the required adjustments before the quantum information is lost due to decoherence.

One prevailing technique in QEC is Shor's Nine-Qubit Code, which allows both bit-flip and phase-flip errors to be corrected. Furthermore, utilizing concatenated coding and fault-tolerant operation designs, quantum error correction codes - like the surface code and the topological code - have been shown to greatly improve the resilience of quantum systems to errors.

Remember, the primary goal of quantum error correction is to protect encoded logical qubits for an arbitrarily long time to enable complex computations. This goal remains a rather ambitious technical challenge.

Please note that QEC is currently a rather active field of research and we have a long way to go towards successful and practical quantum error correction.

6.5 Why is it important to address quantum noise and decoherence in practical quantum computing applications?

Quantum systems differ from classical ones in that they operate based on quantum mechanics principles, notably including superposition and entanglement. As such, quantum computation systems offer the promise of novel computational abilities that far surpass their classical counterparts.

However, these quantum systems are especially susceptible to a variety of errors during computation. These errors can be introduced via unwanted interactions with the environment, resulting in decoherence, or as an intrinsic noise in quantum operations. To comprehend why quantum error correction is essential, let's broadly understand these two primary sources of errors:

1. **Quantum Noise**: Standard operations on quantum gates have intrinsic noise. Imperfections during gate operations and hardware instabilities cause such noise, resulting in errors in computations.

2. **Decoherence**: Quantum systems are known for their delicate features. Interaction between a quantum system and its environment can lead to the loss of quantum coherence, a phenomenon known as decoherence. This interaction collapses the quantum state leading to a loss in information hence a computational error.

Quantum Error Correction (QEC) is designed to protect quantum information from errors due to decoherence and other quantum noise. Without error correction, practically useful quantum computation can be impossible since the cumulative effect of the noise sources mentioned above may ultimately destroy the data. QEC mitigates errors by encoding a logical qubit in a subspace spanned by multiple physical qubits.

The critical importance of QEC is primarily due to the following reasons:

1. **Preservation of Quantum Information**: The encoding of quantum information in quantum error-correcting codes allows the system to preserve quantum information despite errors from decoherence and noise.

2. **Reliable Quantum Computation**: Correcting the errors allows for more reliable quantum computing operations, thus facilitating the practical use of quantum computers.

3. **Scalability**: Quantum error correction is a critical component for the scalability of quantum devices. Without QEC, any attempt to scale quantum devices would result in a high rate of computational

errors, leading to unreliable results. QEC helps in having many qubits while maintaining accurate operations.

In conclusion, quantum error correction is vital for the functioning and development of practical quantum computing applications, ensuring the accuracy and reliability of quantum computations. Despite being a challenging task due to quantum mechanics' probabilistic nature and the no-cloning theorem, effective error correction in quantum systems is an active field of study and a problem being addressed continually.

6.6 What are quantum error correction codes, and why are they important?

Quantum Error Correction Codes (QECCs) are strategies developed to protect quantum information from errors due to decoherence, unwanted interactions with the environment, and other sources of noise. They are an essential component of fault-tolerant quantum computation which will be vital for large scale quantum computing technology.

Classical error correcting codes cannot directly be applied to quantum bits (qubits) because the copying of arbitrary unknown quantum states is not possible due to the quantum no-cloning theorem. Besides, quantum states are continuous and, therefore, are subject to a potentially infinite number of errors, unlike classical bits that can only flip.

These challenge result in the development of QECCs which have a different approach. The basic idea is to encode a qubit into an entangled state of several physical qubits. An encoded qubit is protected from errors because the state of the encoded qubit is spread across these multiple physical qubits - a change in a single physical qubit (from an error) can be detected and corrected without measuring the underlying encoded qubit.

For instance, a simple three-qubit quantum error correction code, called bit flip code, can be used to correct an arbitrary single-qubit error. In this scheme, the quantum state of a single qubit is encoded into the three-qubit state. If an error happens in one of these qubits, we can detect it through carefully designed operations and correct it. The error syndrome is measured without disturbing the encoded quantum state.

QECCs and the development of fault-tolerant protocols are of critical importance for quantum computers to be able to carry out computations with arbitrary precision. They extend the lifetimes of quantum states, they are a form of active noise suppression, and they enable us to handle global system noise through a process of decentralization. Without QCCEs, any current quantum technology will either have its computational power severely limited or operate inaccurately.

Mathematically, a quantum error correction code is specified by a subspace C of the Hilbert space H of a quantum system. To correct errors, one performs a measurement described by a set of projection operators that partition the Hilbert space into orthogonal subspaces, each associated with a unique error. Such a set of projectors is called an error detection measurement. The subspaces are labeled by the binary error vectors, whose components specify which of the error events have occurred.

As a note, developing and implementing effective QECCs is one of the key challenges in the field of quantum computing. However, it's quite promising through strategies like topological codes, color codes, and others that hold promise for practical implementation on large-scale quantum computers.

6.7 How does the concept of redundancy apply in quantum error correction codes?

The concept of redundancy in quantum error correction codes is some-what analogous to the classical concept of redundancy in error correction, but it has a few twists due to the unique principles of quantum mechanics.

In classical error correction, redundancy is used by encoding the original information into longer strings of bits, i.e., your information is not coded into a single bit, but across several bits, so if one fails, you still have information from the other bits. This process is often summarized by the phrase "Don't put all your eggs in one basket".

The same idea carries over into quantum error correction codes. A quantum bit (or qubit), the fundamental unit of quantum information, is not fault-tolerant on its own. Errors due to interaction with the environment—a phenomenon known as "decoherence"—can destroy the state of a qubit. To protect against such errors, quantum error correction codes employ redundancy by encoding the original quantum information of a qubit into a subspace of a larger quantum system involving many physical qubits.

A specific example of a quantum error correction code that uses redundancy is the Shor code, the first quantum error correction code. It encodes 1 logical qubit into 9 physical qubits, effectively spreading out the "information" of the logical qubit across multiple physical qubits, thereby ensuring the information is not lost if an error affects one of the physical qubits.

However, redundancy in the quantum realm must deal with a significant challenge: the "no-cloning" theorem of quantum mechanics, which states it's not possible to make an exact copy of an arbitrary unknown quantum state. Since you can't simply clone quantum states for redundancy, quantum error correction codes don't just rely on replication of information, but also on entanglement and interference. These quantum properties allow quantum error correction codes to detect and correct errors without directly measuring (and thus disturbing) the fragile quantum information.

In summary, redundancy in quantum error correction codes involves distributing the information across multiple qubits to protect it from errors due to decoherence or other factors. Redundancy is achieved not just by replication but also through entanglement and interference, which work to preserve quantum information while respecting the no-cloning theorem of quantum mechanics.

6.8 Can you provide an example of a quantum error correction code?

A commonly used quantum error correction code is the Shor code (also known as the 9-qubit code), which was invented by Peter Shor in 1995. It was the first quantum error-correction code to be discovered and is capable of correcting arbitrary single-qubit errors.

Shor's error correction code uses a block of 9 physical qubits to represent each logical qubit. Hence, it's a [[9,1,3]] code. This means it uses 9 qubits for encoding 1 logical qubit, and it can correct errors of up to 3-bit flip or 3-phase flip.

Let's consider an example.

We start with a single qubit in the state $|\psi\rangle = \alpha|0\rangle + \beta|1\rangle$. The Shor code encodes this qubit state into nine qubits in the state: $|\psi\rangle = \alpha|000\rangle| + ++\rangle + \beta|111\rangle| ---\rangle$

Here, $|+\rangle = \frac{1}{\sqrt{2}}(|0\rangle + |1\rangle)$ and $|-\rangle = \frac{1}{\sqrt{2}}(|0\rangle - |1\rangle))$ to give encoding against phase-flip errors. The encoding state can be expanded as follows: $|\psi\rangle = \frac{1}{2\sqrt{2}}[\alpha(|000\rangle + |111\rangle) + \beta(|000\rangle - |111\rangle)]^{(3)}$

The superscript (3) indicates that the corresponding three-qubit state is repeated three times. This redundancy in the code words contains the necessary information to identify and correct errors.

After the quantum information has been transmitted or manipulated, the recipient can perform a measurement on the received qubits to detect possible errors in the bit values and phases, and therefore correct them.

This is just one example of quantum error correction codes. There are also many other types of error correction codes like Steane code, Surface code, etc. They all work on the same basic principal of redundancy and error detection/correction, but with different efficiencies and robustness against different types of error sources.

6.9 How do quantum error correction codes preserve qubit information?

Quantum error correction codes play a vital role in preserving qubit information from decoherence and other forms of quantum noise, which are inevitable issues in quantum computing. The techniques for quantum error correction are fundamentally different from classical error correction methods due to the unique properties of quantum information, particularly superposition and entanglement.

In a quantum error correction code, qubits are encoded in a way that allows possible errors to be detected and corrected without measuring the qubit states directly, which would destroy the quantum information due to the "no-cloning theorem". The primary roles of a quantum error correction code are to detect any errors that have occurred and then to correct these errors.

One example of quantum error correction code is the well-known Shor Code. If we take a single logical qubit, it can be encoded into 9 physical qubits. To illustrate this further, suppose the state of the logical qubit is given by $\alpha|0_L\rangle + \beta|1_L\rangle$. Then, the Shor Code encodes $|0_L\rangle$ as $|0_L\rangle = (|000\rangle + |111\rangle)^{\otimes 3}$ and $|1_L\rangle$ as $|1_L\rangle = (|000\rangle - |111\rangle)^{\otimes 3}$, where $\otimes$ denotes the tensor product.

This encoding scheme allows the detection and correction of not only bit flip errors $X = \begin{bmatrix} 0 & 1 \\ 1 & 0 \end{bmatrix}$ but also phase flip errors $Z = \begin{bmatrix} 1 & 0 \\ 0 & -1 \end{bmatrix}$.

The error syndrome measurement process involves auxiliary qubits (ancilla qubits) using certain unitary operations and further measurements. Once the type of error and its location are detected, appropriate quantum gate operations (like Pauli X or Z) can be used to correct the errors.

In this way, quantum error correction codes are designed to identify errors and rectify them, preserving the original quantum information. However, these processes require additional resources and increase the complexity of quantum computing systems. Building fault-tolerant quantum computers that can perform reliable quantum error correction is one of the significant challenges at the frontier of quantum computing.

6.10   What challenges are there in implementing quantum error correction codes?

Quantum error correction is a critical area in the field of quantum computing, but it faces many profound challenges. Here are a few key challenges in implementing quantum error correction codes:

1. **Physical Qubits vs Logical Qubits**: For quantum error correction to be effective, each logical qubit (which carries the 'useful' quantum information) needs to be encoded into multiple physical qubits (the ones we physically manipulate in the lab). Thus, the number of required physical qubits to support error correction is significantly larger than the actual quantum data we wish to process. Given that quantum computing hardware is resource-limited right now, this requirement presents a significant challenge.

2. **Fault-tolerant Operations**: Another substantial challenge is the ability to perform operations on the qubits in a fault-tolerant manner. This means that not only the qubits themselves, but also the operations that are performed on them must be resistant to errors. This requires the use of specific fault-tolerant gate libraries, which adds to the complexity and overhead of quantum computations.

3. **Error Thresholds**: There exists a certain threshold for the

error rate below which the quantum error correction can effectively correct errors faster than they occur. However, for many existing quantum systems, the physical qubits' error rates are unfortunately above these thresholds, making quantum error correction ineffective with current technology.

4. **Decoherence**: Quantum states are notoriously fragile, and can easily lose their coherence due to interaction with the surrounding environment. Decoherence processes introduce additional errors in quantum computation, and building systems with long enough coherence times to allow for error correction is a significant challenge.

5. **Correcting Simultaneously Occuring Errors**: Error correction codes can typically correct a small number of errors that occur between successive rounds of error checking and correction. If more errors occur, it is possible that the code will fail to correct them or even misinterpret them as a different type of error, leading to incorrect correction and potential loss of data. Hence, managing and correcting simultaneously occurring errors remains an open challenge.

6. **Overhead costs**: There is a need for additional gates and circuit depth to implement error correction, which can be measured in terms of space and time. The overhead costs grow with the complexity of error-correction codes, and this can limit computational abilities before coherence times are exceeded.

Mathematically, as an example, one of the simplest quantum error correction codes is the Shor's nine-qubit code. In this, a single logical qubit is redundantly encoded across nine physical qubits in such a way that it can correct for arbitrary errors on a single qubit. The encoding circuit of Shor's code can be represented as:

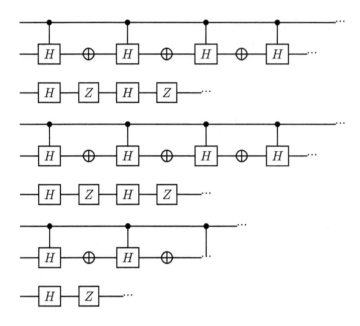

Here, 'H' stands for the Hadamard gate, '@' represents a control gate and 'X', 'Z' represent Pauli gates. These are operations on nine physical qubits to encode a single logical qubit. As you can see, the circuit is not trivial and adds to the overhead of quantum computations.

Thus, the challenges in implementing quantum error correction codes make this an active area of research in the field of quantum computing. Even though we can theoretically define such codes, building them into physical systems remains a nontrivial task.

6.11 What does fault-tolerant quantum computing mean?

Fault-tolerant quantum computing is a property of quantum systems that allows them to continue operating correctly, even in the presence of errors. This is a crucial concept in quantum computing because quantum systems are inherently susceptible to various types of errors, such as bit-flip and phase-flip errors, that can affect the quantum states of qubits (the fundamental unit of quantum information).

In classical computing, we can use parity bits and redundancy techniques to correct errors. However, in quantum computing, things are much more complex due to two key principles of quantum mechanics: superposition and entanglement. Direct copying of quantum information, like in classical error correction schemes, is prohibited by the no-cloning theorem. Therefore, quantum error correction codes (like the Shor code or the surface code) had to be developed to overcome these challenges.

These quantum error correction codes help correct errors by spreading quantum information across multiple physical qubits so that the information can be recovered even if some qubits are error-prone.

Fault-tolerant quantum computing goes a step further by preventing the propagation of errors when quantum gates (the basic operations of quantum computing) are applied. A quantum computer is said to be fault-tolerant if its operations can be performed in a way that does not propagate errors. In other words, the errors that occur do not spread uncontrollably throughout the quantum system, compromising the computational task.

Fault tolerance can be achieved through various methods like magic state distillation, robust initialization and readout procedures, and error-correcting architectures like the surface code that prevent errors from spreading.

Here is an important result in the area of fault-tolerant quantum computing: The threshold theorem states that if the physical error rates of a quantum computer are below a certain threshold, then the computer can simulate an ideal (error-free) quantum computer with arbitrarily small logical error rates, by employing quantum error correction techniques and fault-tolerant procedures.

In conclusion, fault-tolerant quantum computing is the capability of a quantum computer to function correctly in the presence of errors by using specially designed quantum error correction codes and procedures to prevent and correct errors.

Please let me know if you need further details or clarification on this topic.

6.12 Why is fault tolerance crucial in the practical application of quantum computers?

Fault tolerance is crucial in the practical application of quantum computers due to the inherent vulnerability of quantum states to errors. In quantum computing, we work with quantum bits or qubits, whose states are very sensitive and prone to errors from environmental noise or the process of measurements. Such errors are difficult to correct because of the fragile nature of qubit interactions and the no-cloning theorem in quantum mechanics, which says quantum information cannot be copied perfectly.

Fault-tolerant protocols help to counter these errors. They allow quantum computations to continue in the presence of certain errors, without causing the computation to fail. Thus, even though some qubits may flip or phase shift due to environmental interactions or other quantum noises, the quantum computation can still be performed accurately.

Quantum error correction (QEC) codes and fault-tolerant quantum computation methods are designed to diagnose and correct such errors without destroying the quantum information. For example, a common technique used in QEC is redundancy, where the information of one qubit is encoded into a subspace of multiple physical qubits. Any errors affecting these qubits can then be corrected by performing a measurement on all the qubits—this would provide information about the error but not about the encoded information, thereby preserving the quantum states.

Here's an illustrative comparison for a simple 3-qubit repetition QEC code:

Qubit state	Qubit after bit-flip error	Correctable?
000	100	Yes
111	011	Yes

Even if a bit-flip error occurs on any of the qubits, we can identify and correct it because we're encoding the quantum information redundantly across multiple qubits.

However, it's important to note that practical realization of fault-tolerant quantum computation is still a challenging task because it demands very high physical accuracy, often beyond current experimental capabilities.

In summary, fault tolerance is crucial for practical quantum computing because it enables the execution of long sequences of quantum operations with a high enough accuracy, which in turn capable of implementing complex and useful quantum algorithms, despite the presence of error-inducing noise and disturbances.

6.13   How does error correction contribute to fault tolerance in quantum computing?

Quantum Error Correction (QEC) plays a critical role in quantum computing by enabling fault tolerance. Fault-tolerant quantum computing is the idea that errors (or "faults") that occur during quantum computations can be dealt with "on-the-fly." It's the key to practical, large-scale quantum computing, as inevitable quantum noise and other errors can otherwise quickly corrupt quantum states and cause calculations to fail.

Quantum Error Correction helps maintain the integrity of a quantum system by detecting and correcting errors that affect quantum bits or "qubits." This is done using specific quantum error correcting codes, consisting of quantum gates, that can handle the quantum-specific phenomena of superposition and entanglement. These allow the error correction to happen without collapsing the quantum state.

Here's how error correction contributes to fault tolerance in quantum computing:

1. **Error Detection:** Quantum error correcting codes help in identifying the qubits which have been affected by errors. Fault-tolerance requires the ability to detect errors when they occur to effectively correct them.

2. **Error Correction:** Once errors are detected, they need to be corrected to maintain the consistency of the system. Quantum error correction techniques, like the Shor code and Surface codes, can correct a wide variety of common quantum errors without collapsing the quantum state.

3. **Protecting Against Decoherence:** Qubits are sensitive to their environment and tend to lose their quantum characteristics (like superposition and entanglement) over time, a process known as "decoherence." Error correction techniques help prolong the coherence times of qubits, thus enabling functional, fault-tolerant quantum computation.

4. **Preservation of Quantum Information:** Errors, when left uncorrected, can cause loss of important quantum information. Error correction methods not just correct the errors, but also help in maintaining the quantum information during the computation, which is essential for fault tolerance.

5. **Redundancy:** Quantum error correction often involves encoding a "logical qubit" into multiple "physical qubits." This redundancy allows the error correction process to figure out and correct the errors without direct measurement, which would destroy the quantum states.

Importantly, it should be noted that while the theory and preliminary results of QEC are promising, implementing QEC on a large scale in current quantum devices is a significant challenge due to the resource overhead and the need for high-fidelity operations. For truly fault-tolerant quantum computing, it's likely that we'll need to further improve the quality of qubits and quantum gates, invent more efficient error correction techniques, and overcome other technical and material challenges.

6.14 What is the threshold theorem, and how does it relate to fault tolerance?

The Quantum Threshold Theorem (QTT) is one of the most fundamental theorems in quantum information theory. Essentially, it states that if the error rates of physical quantum bits (qubits) and gates in a quantum computer are below a certain threshold, one can perform quantum computations of arbitrary length essentially without error by using quantum error correction (QEC) and fault-tolerant quantum computation.

Just as digital computers can use redundant bits and error-correcting codes to correct for errors, quantum computers can use quantum error-correcting codes to protect against both quantum (phase) and classical errors. However, unlike in classical computers, it is not possible to directly measure and correct the quantum state without destroying the superposition and entanglement of quantum bits.

The Quantum Threshold Theorem proves that if the error per qubit per gate is below a certain value (the threshold), then QEC can be used to suppress the effective error rate to an arbitrarily low level, allowing for reliable quantum computing.

When it comes to fault tolerance, this refers to techniques that allow quantum computers to continue operating and provide correct output even in the presence of errors, just like in classical computing. Fault tolerance is, intrinsically, tied to error correction.

Fault-tolerant quantum computation allows quantum information to be stored, manipulated, and transmitted in such a way that the errors introduced by the 'noise' of the environment and imperfect quantum gates can be corrected faster than they are created.

The threshold error rate for QEC codes is, by definition, the crossover point of a phase transition in the code error rate as a function of the physical gate and qubit errors. If the physical error rates are below the threshold, the code error rate decreases with increasing code distance, and arbitrarily long quantum computations can be executed with arbitrary accuracy. Conversely, if the physical error rates exceed the threshold, then noise propagation due to faulty quantum operations will defeat the error-correcting ability of the QEC code no matter how much redundancy is introduced.

Therefore, the threshold theorem holds the key towards scalable quantum computing since it ensures that, with quantum error-correcting codes and fault-tolerant techniques, we could build a large-scale quantum computer from imperfect and noisy qubits and gates, as long as their error rate is below this threshold value.

Here is an example of a threshold graph:

```
| Physical Error Rate | Code Error Rate |
|---------------------|-----------------|
|      0.0001         |     0.00001     |
|      0.001          |     0.0001      |
|      0.005          |     0.001       |
|      0.01           |     0.01        |
|      0.05           |     0.1         |
|      0.1            |     0.5         |
|      0.2            |     1.0         |
```

Here, the threshold is at a physical error rate of 0.01. If the physical error rate can be reduced below this level, quantum error correction will reduce the effective code error rate below the physical error rate, enabling scalability.

6.15   What are some proposed fault-tolerant quantum computing models?

Sure, several models have been proposed over the years to build fault-tolerant quantum computers. Here some notable ones:

1. **Surface Codes**: These are a type of topological error-correcting code which has garnered much attention due to its high noise threshold (approximately 1%), meaning that if each quantum operation has a probability of error less than this threshold, arbitrarily long quantum computations can be reliably performed. Surface codes are also convenient because their check operators require only nearest-neighbor interactions.

2. **Toric Codes**: Toric codes are a type of quantum error correcting code (QECC) that belongs to the family of topological codes. They are interesting because their error threshold is reasonably high (again, approximately 1%), yielding potential for practical use for building fault-tolerant quantum computers.

3. **Shor's codes**: These are a family of quantum error correcting codes that were the first to be proposed by Peter Shor in 1995. A variant of Shor's code can detect and correct an arbitrary single-qubit error. However, in practice, the number of physical qubits required by Shor's codes is typically larger than some of the other codes on this list.

4. **Steane code**: The Steane code is another notable QECC that corrects active errors. It does so using a combination of seven qubits in total (the original qubit plus six extra ancilla qubits). Like Shor's code, it can correct any single-qubit error.

5. **Bacon-Shor codes**: These codes are a family of quantum error correction codes that represent a compromise of sorts between Shor's codes and the topological codes (they are essentially subsets of the surface code). They are particularly resource efficient and have nice features with respect to transversal gate implementation.

6. **Concatenated Codes**: Concatenated codes are a method of arranging QECCs such that the output of higher level "blocks" of one QECC is fed into the input of another. They permit fault-tolerant computation with smaller overhead, but at the cost of a lower noise threshold.

These models vary on aspects such as error threshold, number of physical qubits needed, complexity of operations, etc. The best choice of fault-tolerant quantum computing model heavily depends on the specific conditions and constraints of your quantum computer.

As a note, all of these models incorporate the idea of redundancy where information is spread across several physical qubit in order to counteract the effect of errors (derived from noise, imperfect operations or loss of coherence). Moreover, these models are built upon the assumption that the noise affecting the qubits is local and not too correlated. If this condition is not met, the effective noise threshold from these models could strongly decrease and additional error mitigation strategies would be required.

Chapter 7

Quantum Computing Hardware

This chapter offers a glimpse into the real-world manifestation of quantum computers. We discuss the leading quantum computing platforms—from superconducting and trapped ion qubits to the theoretical topological qubits—providing insights into the technological race to build scalable quantum systems.

7.1 What are the main types of physical systems used to implement qubits?

Qubits, or quantum bits, are the fundamental units of quantum information, and are implemented in various physical systems for realizing quantum computing. The principal types of physical systems are:

1. Superconducting Circuits

2. Trapped Ions

3. Photonic Systems

4. Topological Qubits

5. Quantum Dots

6. Nuclear Magnetic Resonance (NMR)

7. Diamond Vacancy Centers

1. **Superconducting Circuits**: This is one of the most promising technologies for constructing qubits, and is widely used in quantum computers built by Google, IBM, and other organizations. Qubits are made with superconducting circuits that, when cooled to near absolute zero, allow current to flow indefinitely, thus preserving their quantum states.

2. **Trapped Ions**: In this method, ions are trapped using electromagnetic fields and manipulated using lasers or microwave radiation. The qubits are represented by the internal states of the ions. This method provides very high-fidelity qubits and it's used in quantum computers built by IonQ and Honeywell.

3. **Photonic Systems**: In these systems, qubits are represented by the quantum states of photons. Photonic systems are promising due to the relative ease of manipulating photons and their robustness to environmental noise, however, creating interactions between photon qubits is challenging.

4. **Topological Qubits**: These are still largely theoretical and are yet to be realized in practice. They are expected to have very high error threshold. Microsoft is one of the corporations that are researching this approach.

5. **Quantum Dots**: Quantum dots or semiconductor qubits are another technology which rises as an alternative to superconducting qubits. The advantage of quantum dots is that they can work at higher temperatures than superconductors.

6. **Nuclear Magnetic Resonance (NMR)**: In this method, the spin states of atomic nuclei are used as qubits. This was one of the

initial methods used for quantum computation demonstrations.

7. **Diamond Vacancy Centers**: Here, qubits are represented by the energy states of a missing atom in a diamond lattice.

Each physical implementation has its pros and cons and is at a different stage of development, but it's important to note that we have yet to determine which will be the most scalable/practical for large quantum computers.

To compare the platforms, let's say we have a few criteria such as Scalability, Coherence Time, Gate Speed, and Gate Fidelity which could be represented in a tabular form:

Physical systems	Scalability	Coherence Time	Gate Speed	Gate Fidelity
Superconducting	High	Medium	High	High
Trapped Ions	Medium	High	Low	High
Photonic Systems	Low	High	Medium	Medium
Topological	High	High	Unknown	High
Quantum Dots	High	Medium	Medium	Medium
NMR	Low	Low	Low	Medium
Diamond Vacancy	Low	High	Low	Medium

These characteristics are subject to change as the research and technology progress. Each platform has its unique advantages and suitable applications.

7.2 How does the choice of physical implementation impact the quantum computer's capabilities?

The choice of physical implementation significantly affects the capabilities of a quantum computer in several ways:

1. **Qubit Quality**: The qubit is the basic unit of quantum information, similar to a classical bit but with the added functionality of being in a superposition of states. The quality of a qubit determines

the overall performance and accuracy of a quantum computer.

2. **Scalability**: The physical implementation affects how easily new qubits can be added and how they are connected with each other. Some methods might allow for more compact designs, or easier scalability, while others might provide higher-quality qubits with less scalability.

3. **Coherence Time**: The time during which quantum information can be stored is known as the coherence time. Longer coherence times, which are dependent upon the physical implementation, allows for more complex computations.

4. **Error Rates**: Different physical implementations come with different error rates. Low error rates are crucial for quantum computations because unlike classical computers, quantum errors cannot be rectified without affecting the system as a whole.

5. **Operating Environment**: Some physical implementations require extremely low temperatures, while others might operate at room temperature, or require specific conditions, like certain types of radiation or magnetic fields. This determines the infrastructure needed to maintain the quantum computer.

Here is a comparison of a few physical implementations based on some key parameters:

Depending on the specific needs, one may choose a particular physical implementation for their quantum computing hardware. The area of quantum computations still remains a challenging and highly active field of research.

Qubits Type	Qubit Quality	Scalability	Coherence Time	Error Rates	Operating Environment
Superconducting Circuits	High	Moderate	Short	Low	Very Low temperature
Ion Traps	High	High	Long	High	Room temperature
Topological Qubits	Moderate	High	Extremely Long	Very Low	Requires specific conditions
Photonic Qubits	Low	Low	Short	High	Room temperature

7.3 What challenges exist in developing quantum computing hardware?

There are several significant challenges in the development of quantum computing hardware. I will highlight five of the major ones:

1. **Qubit Quality and Coherence Time**: The quality of a quantum bit (referred as qubit), is one of the most critical factors in quantum computing. A qubit's quality is related to the length of time the qubit can maintain its quantum state, known as the coherence time. Currently, qubits have very short coherence times (typically less than 100 microseconds for superconducting qubits), meaning that computations must be performed very quickly and errors are frequent.

2. **Scaling up Quantum Computers**: Constructing a quantum computer with even a few hundred qubits that can maintain coherence long enough to perform non-trivial computations is a daunting

technological challenge. Existing experimental machines have scaled up to about 50 qubits, but these machines are not yet powerful or reliable enough to outperform classical computers for practical applications.

3. **Quantum Error Correction**: Quantum computers are highly sensitive to environmental noise, which can introduce errors in the computation. Quantum error correction codes can be used to protect against these errors, but they require a significant overhead in the number of physical qubits for each logical qubit. For example, the Surface Code, one of the most common error correction codes, requires approximately 1,000 physical qubits per logical qubit.

4. **Interactions Between Qubits**: Manipulating qubits and transferring information between them without causing decoherence is another significant challenge. In many proposed architectures such as ion traps and superconducting qubits, qubits need to be physically moved or have electrical signals transmitted between them, which can be a source of errors.

5. **Readout and Initialization**: Accurately measuring the state of a qubit without disturbing its quantum nature (readout) and preparing it in a known state (Initialization) is a fundamental challenge.

Here's a table representing these challenges qualitatively

Challenge	Degree of Difficulty
Qubit Quality & Coherence Time	High
Scaling up Quantum Computers	Very High
Quantum Error Correction	Very High
Interactions Between Qubits	High
Qubit Readout & Initialization	Medium

Addressing these challenges will require significant advancements in quantum systems engineering, materials science, and quantum information theory.

7.4   How are qubits physically manipulated in a quantum computer?

Manipulating qubits in a quantum computer involves creating states of superposition, entanglement and performing quantum gates operations. The manipulation technique depends on the physical implementation of the qubits. In practice, several physical implementations exist for qubits, including trapped ions, superconducting circuits, topological quantum computing, and quantum dots. We'll consider two primary examples: superconducting qubits and trapped ion qubits.

1. **Superconducting Qubits**: These are small circuits which contain components called Josephson junctions. Changes in the magnetic flux through these circuits can cause the superconducting current to oscillate between two states, which we can label as $|0\rangle$ and $|1\rangle$. So, manipulation is primarily achieved by applying microwave signals that control this flux.

The Hamiltonian (energy function) of a simple superconducting qubit being driven by an external microwave drive is given by

$$H(t) = \frac{1}{2}(\omega_q - \omega_d)\sigma_z + \frac{1}{2}\Omega(t)\sigma_x$$

where σ_z and σ_x are Pauli matrices, ω_q is the qubit frequency, ω_d is the drive frequency, and $\Omega(t)$ is drive strength or Rabi rate.

In simple terms, you can change the state of the qubit by altering the frequency and strength of the microwaves you're sending through.

2. **Trapped Ion Qubits**: In this system, individual ions are held in traps created by electromagnetic fields, and different energy levels of these ions are used to represent $|0\rangle$ and $|1\rangle$. Manipulation can be achieved by using lasers or microwaves to induce transitions between these energy levels.

$$H(t) = \frac{1}{2}\hbar\omega_0\sigma_z + \hbar\Omega(t)\cos(\omega_d t)\sigma_x$$

Change in energy states per unit time is the angular frequency ω_0, $\Omega(t)$ is the Rabi frequency associated with the interaction strength between the qubit and the driving field, and ω_d is frequency of the driving field.

Other physical realizations of qubits are also possible, and each comes with different techniques for manipulation, as well as different strengths and challenges.

7.5 How do different physical implementations handle issues like decoherence and error correction?

Quantum decoherence and error correction are significant challenges in quantum computing. Let's examine how these issues are addressed in three central physical implementations of quantum computing: Superconducting Circuits, Trapped Ions, and Photonic Quantum Computing.

1. Superconducting Circuits:

In these systems, qubits are formed by storing trapped microwave photons in superconducting loops of metal. Quantum operations are performed by interacting these qubits via shared bus resonators. Superconducting qubits are sensitive to noise since they are made from electronic components. Strategies to handle decoherence are primarily two-fold:

(i) Improving coherence times - This is achieved by engineering the physical qubit and its environment: better materials, better fabrication processes, and smarter qubit designs.

(ii) Error Correction - Quantum error correction codes, like the surface code, can be implemented over a 2D lattice of qubits.

For instance, the transmon qubit, a type of superconducting qubit, can maintain coherence times on the order of 100 microseconds. Recent experiments have shown the feasibility of correcting a bit-flip using quantum error detection with superconducting qubits (Encoding a qubit into a larger two-dimensional Hilbert space of a multi-level system).

2. Trapped Ions:

Here, qubits are stored in the internal states of ions, and gates are realized by shining tightly-focused laser beams on the ions. Trapped ion systems have been demonstrated to have long coherence times (up to several minutes), but they often need to work at cryogenic temperatures to avoid environmental noise. Error correction is carried out using methods analogous to those used in superconducting circuits (surface codes or Shor's codes). A key advantage of trapped ions is that they are all identical, perfect for creating uniform qubits.

3. Photonic Quantum Computing:

This computing model utilizes single photons as qubits, which are manipulated via beam splitters, wave plates, and other optical devices. Photons are robust against decoherence due to their weak interaction with the environment. Also, photonic quantum computation can be performed at room temperature. In the photonic model, error correction is usually not carried out using codes, instead, redundancy is introduced, and a vote among redundant bits is carried out in classical error correction codes.

Here is a high-level comparison:

Please note this is a simplified overview, and each of these implementations has a plethora of nuances and robust research behind them.

Implementation	Approach to Decoherence	Error Correction	Coherence Time
Superconducting Circuits	Improving materials and designs	Quantum error correction codes	100 microseconds
Trapped Ions	Cryogenic conditions	Quantum error correction codes	Several minutes
Photonic	Weak interaction with environment	Classical error correction with redundancies	Not applicable

Table 7.1: Your caption

7.6   What is the principle behind superconducting qubits?

Superconducting qubits, also known as "quantum bits", are at the heart of quantum computing. They are the quantum version of classical bits – whereas classical bits hold a binary value of 0 or 1, quantum bits can hold a value of 0, 1, or both at the same time thanks to the principle of superposition.

The principle behind superconducting qubits lies in the quantum mechanical behavior of an electric circuit. When an electric circuit is cooled to near absolute zero temperatures, it becomes a superconductor and exhibits quantum mechanical effects. Once a circuit is in this superconducting state, we can gather quantum information from it, and that information is stored in the form of qubits.

A qubit has three fundamental properties: superposition, interference and entanglement.

1. Superposition: Unlike classical bits that can exist in state 0 or 1,

a qubit can exist in a superposition of states. This means it can be in state 0, state 1, or any proportion of both. In terms of a Bloch Sphere, this would be represented as a point anywhere on or inside the sphere.

2. Interference: When two qubits are in a state of superposition, they can interfere with each other, much like waves in classical physics. This means that different quantum states can interfere constructively or destructively, and this property is used in quantum algorithms, such as the Quantum Fourier Transform.

3. Entanglement: Two or more qubits can be entangled, meaning that the state of one qubit can instantly affect the state of the other, no matter how far they are separated. This is a key resource for quantum computation and quantum information processing.

A common type of superconducting qubit is the "transmon" qubit, which is a type of charge qubit where the sensitivity to charge noise is reduced, enhancing coherence times. The energy level separation in a transmon qubit is controlled by a Josephson Junction, which allows the precise control necessary for quantum computing.

Overall, the beauty and complexity of superconducting qubits lies in their ability to exist in multiple states simultaneously and to influence each other instantaneously, allowing for incredibly complex computations to happen at certain temperature, exploiting phenomena like quantum superposition and quantum entanglement.

7.7 How are superconducting qubits manipulated and measured?

Superconducting qubits, a type of artificial atom, are one of the leading technologies in Quantum Computing for the implementation of quantum bits, or qubits - the basic units of quantum information.

Manipulating Superconducting Qubits: Manipulation of states in a superconducting qubit is typically achieved through application of microwave pulses. This comes from the fact that the energy difference between the qubit's ground state ('|0>') and its excited state ('|1>') falls into the microwave frequency range.

For example, we could start with a qubit in the ground state '|0>'. Sending a specially prepared microwave pulse would flip the state of the qubit to the excited state '|1>'. The microwave pulses have to be carefully calibrated to achieve the desired manipulations. This idea is the general basis of operations on the qubits.

Measuring Superconducting Qubits: The measurement of superconducting qubits is done through a process called Quantum Non-Demolition (QND) measurement, which allows us to measure without directly disturbing the state of the qubit. In practice, this is done by coupling the qubit to a resonator.

The resonator is used as a kind of quantum bus or line between qubits, and it has its own resonant frequency. When the qubit is in the '|0>' ground state, it shifts the resonator's frequency to a slightly different value than when the qubit is in the '|1>' excited state.

Then, you would send a microwave pulse at the resonator, and, depending on the state of the qubit, the resonator would either reflect or absorb the pulse. By measuring the change in the state of the microwave pulse after it interacts with the resonator, you can deduce the state of the superconducting qubit.

Here is a simple illustration:

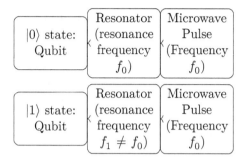

In each case, the microwave pulse after interaction with the resonator will be different. This allows you infer the state of the qubit. Hence, even though the qubit state is not directly disturbed during measurement in Quantum Non-Demolition measurement, its state still impacts the output of the measurement process.

Lastly, remember that even though you can measure a qubit's state, the act of doing so brings it out of superposition due to what we call the Observer Effect. After measurement, the qubit is in either $|0>$ or $|1>$. The superposition state only continues to exist as long as no one tries to measure it. This is one of the key principles behind Quantum Mechanics and Quantum Computing.

7.8 What are the main advantages and disadvantages of superconducting qubits?

Superconducting qubits form the essence of hardware for many types of quantum computers, including those manufactured by Google and IBM. These qubits are artificial atoms built with superconducting electrical circuits.

Advantages:

1. Scalability: Superconducting qubits are microscale circuits, which are compatible with the lithographic techniques used in the semiconductor

industry. This means they have the potential to be produced and scaled in a similar way to classical processors.

2. Customizability: Unlike natural atoms, artificial superconducting atoms can be designed with a wide range of properties (energy levels, decay rates, coupling strengths, etc.). Thus, you can optimize or adapt the properties of the quantum system based on the requirements of the application at hand.

3. Strong Interactions: Superconducting qubits can couple strongly to electromagnetic modes of open transmission lines or to each other directly, opening up a huge range of potential applications in quantum simulation, computation, and metrology.

4. Design Improvements: Over the years, better designs and materials have led to consistent improvements in coherence times.

However, superconducting qubits also have their challenges:

Disadvantages:

1. Decoherence: Quantum properties are very delicate. Errors can result from the interaction of qubits with their environment. While decoherence times have improved, qubit quality is still a major concern.

2. Quality Variability: There can be variability in qubit quality and control. Not all qubits are equal, and sometimes implementing multiple qubits with uniform quality can be challenging.

3. Readout Errors: Reading the state of a qubit can cause problems. This is because qubits need to interact with a measurement device, but if there's an exchange of energy, the qubit's state can be changed.

4. Error Correction: As with all quantum systems, superconducting qubits need error correction techniques to make practical, large-scale quantum computation possible, and these techniques are still being developed.

5. Cooling Needs: Superconducting circuits need to be cooled down to ultra-cold temperatures (around 10 millikelvin), limiting their prac-

tical usage.

In summary, the superconducting qubits pave a path toward building a large-scale quantum computer, but several challenges need to be overcomed before turning this potential into a reality.

7.9 How do superconducting qubits handle quantum decoherence?

Superconducting qubits tackle quantum decoherence, or 'noise', through several techniques, including:

1. **Error Correction Codes**: To counteract the problem of quantum decoherence, quantum error correction codes are used. These allow the system to manage errors without knowing their exact nature. One popular example is the Surface Code, specifically tailored for systems like superconducting qubits where "bit-flip" and "phase-flip" errors can occur.

2. **Qubit Design and Material Improvement**: Superconducting qubits implement a multitude of designs such as transmon qubits, Xmons, and gmon qubits. These designs exhibit longer coherence times (35 to 150 μs) through mitigation of unwanted electromagnetic modes. For instance, the transmon qubits are less sensitive to charge noise because of their nonlinear interaction between microwave radiation and quantized electrical circuits. Similarly, improvements in materials used can help reduce noise.

3. **Cryogenics**: Superconducting qubits operate in cryogenic environments, typically at temperatures below 1 Kelvin. This extremely low temperature helps to minimize thermal fluctuations, reducing the chance of qubits' quantum state being disrupted.

4. **Qubit Isolation**: The isolation of qubits can also reduce decoherence by minimizing their interaction with other quantum systems. This can be accomplished by implementing careful shielding of qubits

and reducing the cross-talk between adjacent lines.

For instance, if we take the example of the IBM Quantum system, superconducting qubits are within a "fridge" (dilution refrigerator) that operates at 15 milliKelvin, effectively isolating the qubits from the environment and reducing decoherence.

Here is a general representation of how quantum decoherence affects superconducting qubits and their mitigation strategies:

Table 7.2: Mitigation in Superconducting Qubits

Decoherence Sources	Mitigation in Superconducting Qubits
Thermal Fluctuations	Operating at cryogenic temperatures
Charge Noise	Usage of Transmon qubits design
Quantum Errors (bit flip, phase flip)	Application of Quantum Error Correcting Codes
Interaction with environment	Careful shielding and isolation of qubits

It's worth noting that, despite these mitigations, quantum decoherence remains a challenging problem for superconducting qubits, and ongoing research is targeted towards improving qubit design, control, and operation to further tackle decoherence.

7.10 How are superconducting qubits used in building large-scale quantum systems?

Superconducting qubits are a type of artificial atom fabricated from electrical circuit components. They are the key building blocks of large-scale quantum systems used in quantum computing. Their design incorporates the principles of quantum mechanics to allow them to operate in a quantum state. Superconducting qubits have made considerable progress in terms of controllability and coherence times, which are critical for the development of quantum computing.

At its core, a superconducting qubit here involves a simple LCR resonant circuit which consists of a Josephson junction (which plays the role of an inductor), a capacitor (C), and a resistor (R) which is usually ignored because the circuit behaves in a superconducting state.

There are different types of superconducting qubits, such as charge qubits, flux qubits, and phase qubits. Nowadays, the most commonly used design is the transmon qubit because of its robustness to noise.

Here is how these qubits are used in building large-scale quantum systems:

1. **Qubit Coupling:** To build large-scale quantum computational systems, we need to couple these qubits, thus enabling quantum gates and algorithm implementation. Qubits can be coupled directly, through the use of a common resonator or bus, or using tunable couplers.

2. **Error Correction:** Large-scale quantum systems must also employ quantum error correction codes to correct for errors due to environmental noise and imperfections in quantum gates. A common strategy involves encoding a logical qubit into multiple physical qubits.

3. **Control and Readout:** Each qubit in a quantum processor is individually controllable and measurable. Qubit control is usually achieved through microwave pulses, and measurement is performed by bringing the qubit into resonance with a readout resonator.

4. **Scalability:** The design of superconducting qubits allows them to be manufactured using well-established microfabrication techniques, ensuring scalability to large systems.

Here's an example circuit:

This represents a superconducting qubit circuit with a Josephson junction ('JJ') and capacitor ('C').

Overall, building a large-scale quantum system using superconducting qubits is a complex task that requires a balanced approach to qubit design, error correction, control, readout, and ultimately the ability to fabricate and operate a well-controlled multilayer system at low temperatures. However, by continuously improving and developing new technologies, we are making steady progress towards this goal.

7.11 What are trapped ion qubits and how do they work?

Trapped ion qubits are one of the promising candidates for the physical implementation of quantum bits (qubits), the basic units of information in quantum computing.

In a trapped ion quantum computer, single atomic ions are isolated and held in place by electromagnetic fields in an ultra-high vacuum apparatus. Each atomic ion provides a pristine qubit that can be easily manipulated and read out using lasers or microwave radiation. An advantage of trapped ions is that, because it is a naturally occurring quantum object, no fabrication process is needed to make the qubits.

Here's a basic workflow of how they operate:

1. **Qubit Initialization**: Each qubit is initialized to a well-defined state (often the lowest energy state, which we will call the '0' state). This can be accomplished by cooling the trapped ion system close to absolute zero.

2. **Qubit Manipulation**: Qubits in the system can be manipulated by applying laser or microwave radiation. This allows individual qubits to be manipulated into the desired state. You can represent any quantum state of a single qubit using the Bloch sphere model as follows:

$$|\psi\rangle = \cos(\theta/2)|0\rangle + e^{i\phi} \sin(\theta/2)|1\rangle$$

where ' ' and ' ' determine the direction of the quantum state vector on the Bloch sphere, representing any superposition of basis states '0' and '1'.

3. **Qubit Interaction**: Extremely well-tuned laser pulses can make two qubits interact, for instance to perform a controlled-NOT gate operation. If the first qubit is in the state '1', then the second qubit will be flipped. But if the first qubit is in the '0' state, then the second qubit does nothing. These interactions are key to many quantum algorithms.

4. **Qubit Measurement**: Reading the state of a qubit can be done through state-dependent fluorescence. If the qubit is in the '1' state, it will scatter lots of photons and appear bright when illuminated with a particular laser, but if it's in the '0' state it will scatter hardly any photons and appear dark.

The ion-trap quantum computer proves to be an excellent choice due to its long coherence times, high-fidelity readout, single-qubit addressability, and the ability to entangle multiple qubits. The most significant challenge for scalability is to maintain these characteristics in larger systems, particularly those that use transport for two-qubit operations. Despite such challenges, trapped ion technology remains one of the most promising paths to constructing practical quantum computer systems.

7.12   What are the main benefits and drawbacks of trapped ion qubits?

The topic of quantum computing continues to be a significantly exciting field of study, with multiple different quantum computing technologies being explored. One of the vital avenues is the usage of trapped ion qubits - atomic ions confined and isolated by electromagnetic fields.

Benefits of Trapped Ion Qubits

1. **High Qubit Quality**: In comparison to other quantum computers, trapped ion systems have boasted some of the best qubits to date. They have exceptionally long coherence times because the qubits are stored in the internal states of the ions which can be very well isolated from the environment.

2. **Fully-Connected Qubits**: This is one of the major practical advantages of trapped ions. Unlike some other forms of quantum processing units, which require physical movement or complex optical setups to create different connections, trapped ion devices naturally have all-to-all connectivity because ions in the trap can be directly coupled via their Coulomb interaction.

3. **High Precision Operations**: Since ions are almost identical in charge and mass, we can manipulate them with a high degree of precision. Laser light is often used as a control mechanism, enabling extraordinarily precise operations.

4. **Mature Technology**: Trapping ions is a well-established technique in physics, and the basic science and engineering of these systems are well-understood.

Drawbacks of Trapped Ion Qubits

1. **Scalability Issues**: One of the significant challenges for trapped ion qubits is in managing scalability, primarily when using traditional methods that use ion chains in single linear traps. As more ions are

added into a linear trap, they become more difficult to control, which can lead to errors.

2. **Slower Operations**: Compared to other quantum computing technologies, trapped ions should have slower gate operations, mainly due to the slow speed at which the quantum information is transferred between qubits, which is mediated by the vibrational motion of the ions.

Summary Table:

Table 7.3: Benefits and Drawbacks of Trapped Ion Qubits

	Trapped Ion Qubits
Benefits	High-Qubit Quality, Full Connectivity, High-Precision Operations, Mature Technology
Drawbacks	Scalability Issues, Slower Operations

In summary, trapped ion qubits offer some compelling strengths, with excellent qubit quality and intrinsic full-connectivity being the major ones. However, the issues of scalability and slow operations are key challenges that need to be overcome for the realization of large-scale trapped-ion quantum computers.

7.13 How are qubit states manipulated in trapped ion systems?

In trapped ion quantum computing systems, the manipulation of qubit states is achieved through two main processes: laser or microwave interactions and quantum gates through entanglement.

1. **Laser or Microwave Interactions:**

Individual ions (qubits) in a string are manipulated using focused laser beams or microwaves. By adjusting the frequency, duration, and phase of the radiation, precise operations can be performed on the quantum state of the ions.

The interaction between radiation and atoms or ions can be described using the Hamiltonian formalism. The Hamiltonian H that describes the interaction of an atom with an external electromagnetic field (in dipole approximation) is

$$H = H_0 - \mu \cdot E.$$

Here, H_0 is the Hamiltonian in the absence of external field, μ is the atomic dipole moment, and E is the electric field strength. The electric field can be expressed as a superposition of sinusoidal plane waves. Plugging this into the Hamiltonian and solving the resulting equations leads to the phenomenon of Rabi oscillations, which forms the basis for state manipulation in trapped ion systems.

2. **Quantum Gates through Entanglement:**

Entanglement is a uniquely quantum mechanical resource that is used to perform two-qubit logic gates. In trapped ion systems, entanglement is created by applying laser pulses that couple to the collective motion of the ions, creating entangled states.

The entanglement of two qubits ("ion 1" and "ion 2") can schematically be described like this:

- Start with both qubits in the ground state, i.e., the initial state is $|g\rangle_1|g\rangle_2$.

- Apply a laser pulse to ion 1 that, for example, puts it into a superposition of ground and excited state, $1/\sqrt{2}(|g\rangle_1 + |e\rangle_1)|g\rangle_2$.

- Because of the coupling to the collective motion, the state after the pulse becomes $1/\sqrt{2}(|g\rangle_1|g\rangle_2 + |e\rangle_1|e\rangle_2)$. Now the two ions are entangled.

- Applying suitably designed pulses to one or both ions can now be used to carry out arbitrary two-qubit logic gates. These gates form the basis of universal quantum computing.

The precise control and isolation of trapped ions from their environment make them excellent systems for the manipulation of qubit states in quantum computing. However, engineering challenges related to scaling up these systems to many qubits remain.

7.14 How does decoherence manifest in trapped ion systems, and how is it mitigated?

Decoherence in trapped ion systems is mainly affected by three key factors:

1) **Heating of the Ion Trap Modes:** When the ions in the trap interact with the environment, heat is introduced into the system, increasing thermal instability of the trap modes. These modes are responsible for interactions between ions and thus crucial for quantum gate operations. Heating therefore introduces errors into quantum computations. It is currently the most significant source of error in trapped ion qubits.

2) **Decoherence due to Inelastic Scatter:** Quantum computing in trapped ion systems utilizes lasers for qubit state manipulation. During these processes, scattering can occur – either elastic, which only changes the direction of the photon, or inelastic, which changes the energy/phase of the ion. Inelastic scatter causes quantum state decoherence, introducing errors into quantum computations.

3) **Spontaneous Emission:** Due to interaction with the environment, an ion in an excited state can fall to its ground state spontaneously, emitting its excess energy as a photon. Spontaneous emission is a source of uncontrollable decoherence and associated quantum errors.

To mitigate these issues, various strategies can be used:

- For reducing the effects of heating, improved trap designs and materials, operating at cryogenic temperatures and advances in qubit operations like using higher optical wavelengths can be employed.

- Decoherence due to inelastic scatter can be reduced by choosing ion species with small inelastic scattering cross sections and/or operating at wavelengths where the cross section is small. Calibration routines can also be used to compensate for the phase changes.

- Spontaneous emission can be minimized by choosing appropriate qubit energy level configurations (like using hyperfine levels in ground state with longer coherence times) and reducing operational times, such that less spontaneous emission has time to occur.

Quantum error correction and fault-tolerant codes can also be used to combat errors caused by decoherence. By encoding logical qubits into larger sets of physical qubits and applying error detecting/correcting gates, quantum computation can still proceed accurately despite individual qubits experiencing decoherence.

In summary, while there are challenges in trapped ion quantum computing due to decoherence, several techniques can mitigate this factor to make quantum computations reliable and feasible in real-world operations.

7.15   How are trapped ion systems used in the construction of larger quantum computers?

Trapped ion systems serve as one of the leading platforms for scalable quantum computing. The central idea is to utilize individual ions (charged atoms) as quantum bits (qubits), the fundamental units of information in a quantum computer.

Here's a high-level overview of how it works:

1. **Ion Trapping:** The ions are trapped using electromagnetic fields in a vacuum chamber. Lasers are then used to cool these ions down. The ions hover in the same location due to the effect of the trapping fields and their mutual Coulomb repulsion. These ions, which can be individual atoms like Ytterbium or Calcium, are used as qubits.

2. **Qubit Initialization:** Each ion's electronic state is initialized using a laser pulse, setting up the starting computational basis.

3. **Quantum Gate Operations:** Quantum logic gates (analogous to classical logic gates) are then applied using finer, targeted laser pulses. This manipulates the quantum state of the qubits. Two-qubit gates can leverage the Coulomb interaction between ions, which can be controlled by applying the appropriate laser pulses. This is a crucial aspect for quantum computing.

4. **Qubit Readout:** The quantum state of each qubit is measured by scattering many photons from it, with the resulting fluorescence determining the final state of the qubit.

The aim in trapped ion systems, like all quantum computing systems, is to perform these operations while minimizing the effect of errors and noise to maintain the quantum coherence of the system for as long as possible. Long coherence times, high-fidelity gate operations, and the potential for full-connectivity between qubits are some benefits of trapped ion systems.

For instance, all ions in the chain can interact with each other, increasing the ease and efficiency with which multi-qubit operations can be performed, compared to some other quantum computing technologies.

One of the challenges so far has been scaling the system with large numbers of ions, as handling, manipulating, and reading large numbers of ions in a single chain become harder. State-of-the-art techniques are addressing this by attempting to link multiple smaller chains using photons, forming a modular, larger quantum computer.

This diagram provides a illustration of a small trapped ion system:

```
Ion: Qubit
Laser: Gate   Laser Interference
Trap: Field   Electromagnetic Trap
```

Each ion in the chain represents a qubit; lasers provide the mechanism for qubit initialization, quantum gate operations, and readout; and the whole system remains confined and well controlled within the electromagnetic trap.

Nonetheless, realizing a large, practical quantum computer is a significant challenge that will require continued advancements and innovations in trapped ion technology.

Chapter 8

Current and Future Applications of Quantum Computing

Here, we explore the exciting range of applications that quantum computing promises. From cryptography and material science to solving complex optimization problems, we discuss how quantum computing has the potential to revolutionize various fields and glimpse into the future possibilities.

8.1 How could quantum computing potentially disrupt current encryption techniques?

Quantum computing promises not just advances in scientific computing, but also the potential to disrupt current encryption techniques, primarily due to its inherent capabilities that conventional computers do not have.

Currently, encryption is based on mathematical problems that are easy to solve in one direction but difficult to compute reversely. Essentially, if you know some prime numbers, it's easy to multiply them together to create a large number, but if you're given just the large number, it's quite difficult to factor it back into the original prime numbers especially when this number gets very long. This is called the factoring problem. This approach is used in RSA encryption, which is currently one of the most popular encryption methods.

Quantum computing, however, threatens this due to a quantum algorithm known as Shor's algorithm. Shor's algorithm can factorize numbers more efficiently than classical computers, due to the phenomena of quantum superposition and entanglement. In theoretical terms, a large enough quantum computer running Shor's algorithm could break RSA encryption keys with ease, thereby making traditional encryption methods unsafe.

Mathematically, while a classical computer factors a number 'N' in $O((logN)^2(loglogN)(logloglogN))$ using the best current algorithms like general number field sieve, a quantum computer can factor 'N' in $O((logN)^3)$ operations using Shor's algorithm. This implies an exponential speedup which demonstrates the threat to current encryption techniques.

Now, the caveat to all of this is that currently practical quantum computers capable of running Shor's algorithm against encryption keys of meaningful length do not yet exist. However, anticipating this, research is already underway to design and implement so-called "post-quantum cryptography". These cryptographic techniques should be secure against both quantum and classical computers, and even remain secure in the presence of a quantum computer.

8.2 What is quantum cryptography, and how could it provide superior security?

Quantum cryptography, specifically quantum key distribution (QKD), is a method for secure communication that allows two parties to produce a shared random secret key known only to them, which can then be used to encrypt and decrypt their private messages. This technique takes advantage of the quantum mechanical properties of particles like photons to secure data transmission.

In theoretical terms, quantum cryptography offers superior security to classical cryptography due to its fundamental properties. This can be summarized as follows:

1. **Uncertainty Principle:** In quantum mechanics, you cannot measure a quantum state without disturbing it. If an eavesdropper tries to intercept the quantum signal in QKD, they inevitably alter the state of the transmitted photon. This disturbance can be detected by the sender and receiver, allowing them to know if their key transmission has been intercepted, providing a secure key exchange.

2. **No Cloning Theorem:** It states one cannot create an identical copy of an arbitrary unknown quantum state. So even if eavesdropper intercepts a photon from the quantum signal, they can't reproduce it to send an identical photon to the receiver without the receiver detecting the interception.

3. **Quantum Entanglement:** This is another powerful principle used in quantum cryptography. Entangled quantum particles exhibit highly correlated properties, even when separated by vast distances. Attempt to observe or measure an entangled property disrupts the entanglement, and this disruption can also be detected.

Current uses of quantum cryptography are not widespread, due to the need for specialized equipment (such as quantum enabled fiber-optic lines or satellites) and the substantial computational resources required. However, it is likely that as quantum technology continues to mature, QKD will start to play a key role in securing sensitive communications against potential quantum-computing based attacks in the future.

In the conventional RSA cryptosystem, for instance, modern computers would take an exponentially long time to factor large numbers used as keys. However, a sufficiently powerful quantum computer using Shor's algorithm could achieve this much faster, compromising many current encryption schemes. As quantum computing advances, quantum cryptography, using QKD, becomes an increasingly necessary solution to ensure communication security.

8.3   How does Shor's algorithm impact current cryptographic techniques?

Shor's algorithm, formulated by the mathematician Peter Shor in 1994, profoundly impacts the field of cryptography, particularly public-key cryptographic systems such as RSA and elliptic curve algorithms.

Public-key cryptography relies on the mathematical challenge of factoring large prime numbers to provide security. Classical computers currently can't factor a large enough product of primes before the heat death of the universe, which in effect renders these encryption systems secure.

However, Shor's algorithm leverages the principles of quantum computing to efficiently factor large numbers. It essentially transforms the problem of factoring into a problem of period-finding for which a quantum computer has a massive advantage, and as a result, it can potentially break many types of encryption that are currently used.

To illustrate the impact, classical algorithms for factoring are exponential in nature, with time complexity growing exponentially with the size of the number to be factored. In contrast, Shor's quantum algorithm for factoring has polynomial time complexity, specifically

it is $O((logN)^3)$, where N is the number to be factored. This difference implies that as soon as practical quantum computers become
available, public key cryptosystems like RSA could be broken.

That's not to say that quantum computers will instantly obliter-
ate all current cryptographic techniques. There has been significant
progress in the direction of "post-quantum cryptography" with some
algorithms believed to remain secure even in a world with quantum
computers, but the implementations are few and not yet widespread.

Shor's algorithm, therefore, underscores the need for a shift toward
these cryptographic techniques that can resist quantum computing
attacks. These potentially include lattice-based cryptography, code-
based cryptography, multivariate polynomial cryptography, and others.

Further research and advancement in quantum computing technology
will give a clearer picture of what exactly this impact might look
like. For now, the best we can do is adequately prepare and build
cryptography methods robust in the age of quantum computing.

8.4   What are the challenges of implement-
ing quantum cryptography in practice?

Quantum cryptography is a promising field that represents one of
the practical applications of quantum computing. It uses the properties of quantum mechanics to establish secure communication channels. Specifically, the quantum key distribution (QKD) technology
is practically unbreakable as it relies on the fundamentals of quantum physics where measuring a quantum system disturbs the system.
Nevertheless, there are several challenges related to its practical implementation.

1. **Quantum Transmission and Fiber Optics Limitations:** Quantum computers communicate using quantum bits (qubits). When
qubits are sent over long distances, they tend to degrade due to en-

vironmental interferences, a problem known as decoherence. Right now, qubits can only be sent a few hundred kilometers over fiber optic cables before they degrade, limiting their use in broader networks.

2. **Scalability:** Modern cryptography techniques can support millions of users. To replicate this using quantum cryptography would require a scalable, and cost-effective infrastructure that can support a large number of users, which is currently a challenge.

3. **Quantum Computer Availability and Cost:** Even though there has been significant progress in the development of quantum computers, there's a lack of fully-functional, error-free quantum computers available to the public, plus they are expensive and require highly specialized personnel to operate, posing a serious limitation to widespread implementation.

4. **Technological Maturity:** Quantum cryptography is a relatively new field, compared to classical cryptography, and the technology is not fully mature. Plus, there are a considerable amount of technical hurdles, like error correction and qubit quality/quantity, to overcome.

5. **Reconciling Quantum and Classical Systems:** Since most systems are currently classically-based, integrating quantum cryptography mechanisms into these systems is challenging, as quantum and classical systems obey fundamentally different laws of physics.

6. **Security of Actual Implementation:** Even though quantum cryptography has theoretical security guarantees, implementation can inadvertently introduce security threats, just like any other software or hardware technology.

In summary, here's a table showing the challenges:

Please note, the field of quantum cryptography is actively researched and advancements are being made to resolve these challenges. Quantum repeaters and satellites for instance are being explored to address the transmission limitations. Similarly, research is ongoing to develop more robust, scalable, and cost-effective quantum technologies.

Table 8.1: Challenges in Quantum Computing

Challenges	Detail
Quantum Transmission and Fiber Optics Limitations	Qubits degrade when transmitted over long distances
Scalability	Lack of scalable quantum infrastructure
Quantum Computer Availability and Cost	Few error-free quantum computers; High cost; Require specialized operation
Technological Maturity	In its relative infancy compared to classical cryptography
Reconciliation between Quantum and Classical Systems	Integrate quantum cryptography mechanisms into classical systems
Security of Actual Implementation	Security threats due to potential vulnerabilities during implementation

8.5 How could a post-quantum cryptography landscape look?

In order to answer your question, it's essential to have an understanding of how quantum computers could potentially disrupt current cryptographic systems.

The most notable impact pertains to public key cryptosystems. In particular, Shor's algorithm, when run on a sufficiently large quantum computer, could crack many of the cryptographic protocols currently in use such as RSA (Rivest-Shamir-Adleman) and ECC (Elliptic-Curve Cryptography).

Therefore, post-quantum cryptography (PQC) is being developed to withstand potential quantum computing threats. The goal is to design cryptographic systems that would remain secure even in the presence of quantum computers.

The post-quantum cryptography landscape may include:

1. **Lattice-based cryptography**: This cryptographic method involves lattices (point-based structures in multiple dimensions). Problems related to finding the shortest paths in lattices (such as the Shortest Vector Problem) are believed to be secure against quantum attacks.

2. **Code-based cryptography**: This approach uses coding theory which involves encoding messages to withstand errors. The security of these systems often relies on the difficulty of decoding a general linear code, which has been shown not to be solvable by a quantum computer in polynomial time.

3. **Multivariate polynomial cryptography**: These schemes base their security on the difficulty of solving systems of multivariate polynomials over finite fields. So far, quantum computers have no demonstrated advantage in solving these problems.

4. **Hash-based cryptography**: Hash functions are another foundation upon which to build quantum-resistant cryptographic systems. The beauty of hash-based systems is their simplicity and the fact that their security is easy to understand.

In a nutshell, the future of post-quantum cryptography looks rich with potential as researchers continue to develop a variety of methods for maintaining secure communications in a world with quantum computers.

One important aspect to keep in mind is that data encrypted today could still be at risk in the future when larger, more powerful quantum computers become a reality. Therefore, sensitive data should be re-encrypted using post-quantum cryptographic methods as an added protective measure.

To summarise, here's a table listing the various post-quantum cryptographic approaches:

Table 8.2: Cryptographic Approaches

Cryptographic Approach	Based On
Lattice-based Cryptography	Hardness of problems in lattices
Code-based Cryptography	Difficulty of decoding a general linear code
Multivariate Polynomial Cryptography	Difficulty of solving systems of multivariate polynomials
Hash-based Cryptography	Simplicity and security of hash functions

8.6 How can quantum computing aid in drug discovery?

Quantum computing, with its vastly superior computational capabilities compared to classical computing, has significant potential to revolutionize the field of drug discovery.

At present, the drug discovery process is quite time and resource-intensive. It can take years or even decades to research and develop a new drug, and costs can run into the billions of dollars. Quantum computing has the potential to drastically cut down on both the time and cost.

This is possible because quantum computing holds the potential to more accurately simulate molecular interactions, a crucial factor behind drug discovery. Allow me to explain:

1. Molecular simulation: The conventional way of modelling interactions between molecules often requires making certain simplifications that can lead to significant errors. Quantum computers, on the other hand, can model these interactions in a more accurate and sophisticated manner. The key point here is that quantum computers can simulate quantum systems, like molecules, natively. They don't need to make approximations.

2. High dimensional problems: In pharmacology, handling high-

dimensional problems, such as protein folding, is always a challenge
due to the exponential increase in complexity. Quantum computing,
with its ability to perform many calculations simultaneously, could
offer a solution here.

3. Speed: Quantum computers can process massive amounts of data
and perform computations at a much faster rate than classical computers. This acceleration could drastically cut down on the time it
takes to discover new drugs.

For instance, companies like IBM and Google are already working on
projects that use quantum computing for drug discovery. IBM, in its
Quantum for Business initiative, has announced it is working with
pharmaceutical companies to find new drugs using quantum computing.

Here is a hypothetical example on how quantum computing can help
in drug discovery:

Without Quantum Computing	With Quantum Computing
Classical molecular simulations conducted	Quantum-based molecular simulations conducted
Takes several years for drug discovery	Takes significantly less time for drug discovery
Faces issues with high-dimensional problems	Handles high-dimensional problems better
Has to deal with approximations	Minimizes need for approximations

In conclusion, quantum computing definitely holds the promise to
revolutionize multiple industries, including the field of drug discovery.
However, it's important to remember that the field is still in nascent
stages, and a lot of research is required before we can fully exploit its
potential.

8.7 What are the potential impacts of quantum computing in materials science?

Quantum computing has significant potential implications in materials science. The fundamental premise lies in its ability to solve complex mathematical problems and simulate physical systems much faster than traditional computers. It is particularly anticipated that the simulation of quantum systems, which is vital for understanding material properties at the atomic and subatomic levels, will be dramatically advanced by quantum computation. Here are some potential impacts:

1. **Accelerated Material Design:** Quantum computers can potentially simulate and analyze a broad array of molecular configurations in a substantially surpassed time compared to classical computers. This acceleration would revolutionize the discovery and design of new materials with desired properties.

2. **Quantum Materials:** Quantum computation can help facilitate the development and understanding of quantum materials, such as superconductors and topological insulators. These properties are inherently quantum mechanical and are challenging to simulate on traditional computers.

3. **Material Optimization:** Quantum computing can be applied to optimize the structure or process for the synthesis or manufacture of particular materials. Such optimization is usually computationally intensive and can be carried out more efficiently using quantum algorithms.

4. **Drug Discovery:** In the realm of biophysical materials science, quantum computers can simulate protein folding and drug interaction in ways that even supercomputers cannot. This could vastly expedite the process of discovering new drugs.

Here is a simple table outlining these applications:

Impact Area	Application in Material Science
Accelerated Material Design	Simulate, analyze molecular configurations, revolutionize the discovery and design of new materials
Quantum Materials	Facilitate the development and understanding of superconductors and topological insulators
Material Optimization	Optimize the structure or process for material synthesis or manufacture
Drug Discovery	Simulate protein folding and drug interaction, expedite drug discovery processes

The development of quantum computing and its application in material science is still in an early stage. However, with rapid advancements and collaborative efforts, quantum computers could dramatically enhance our ability to design, understand, and optimize materials in the near future.

8.8   How could quantum simulations accelerate the discovery process in these fields?

Quantum computing can significantly accelerate the process of discovery in many fields by offering enormous computational power, allowing for the simulation of complex quantum systems that cannot be studied or understood through classical computers. This is particularly important in fields such as:

1. **Drug and Materials Discovery**: Quantum simulations can be used to computationally model molecules in order to understand their

properties and potential use in drug discovery or material science. For instance, it would be possible to model the exact behavior of a drug interacting with a complex protein or to design new materials with desired properties.

For instance, we can write the molecular Hamiltonian suitable for the quantum simulation in the second quantization notation as follows:

$$H = \sum_{ij} c e^{ij} a_i^\dagger a_j + \frac{1}{2} \sum_{ijkl} v^{ijkl} a_i^\dagger a_j^\dagger a_k a_l$$

where $a_i^\dagger$ and a_j are the fermionic creation and annihilation operators respectively, c^{ij} and v^{ijkl} represent the one and two-electron integrals.

2. **Cryptography and Security**: Quantum computers can be used to enhance the security of information transmitted over the internet. Quantum key distribution protocols, like the BB84 protocol, which use the principles of quantum mechanics, ensure that an eavesdropper cannot intercept a key exchange without the knowledge of both parties involved.

3. **Optimization Problems**: Many practical problems, such as supply chain optimization, traffic optimization, or financial modeling, can be framed as complex optimization problems. Quantum computing can potentially solve such optimization problems faster than classical algorithms.

4. **Artificial Intelligence and Machine Learning**: Quantum computing can provide exponential speedup for machine learning algorithms, allowing the processing of a larger amount of data in less time. Also, quantum algorithms such as Quantum Principal Component Analysis (QPCA) provide exponential speedup compared to their classical counterparts.

Quantum simulations are mostly theoretical and experimental at this stage but their potential impact on these fields is significant. However, realizing these promises requires progress in developing scalable,

fault-tolerant quantum computers and creating efficient quantum algorithms for these applications.

8.9   How can quantum computing help solve optimization problems more efficiently?

Quantum Computing's ability to solve optimization problems more
effectively stems from two key features:

1. Quantum Superposition

2. Quantum Entanglement

Let's understand these in detail:

1. Quantum Superposition: In classical computing, a bit can exist
in one of two states: 0 or 1. In contrast, a qubit (quantum bit) can
simultaneously exist in multiple states. This property, known as superposition, allows for a more parallel way of computing. This means
that, for an optimization problem, a quantum computer can evaluate
many more possibilities simultaneously than classical computers.

2. Quantum Entanglement: When qubits are entangled, the state
of one cannot be described independently of the others. This helps
quantum computers to achieve quicker optimization, as changes in
one qubit will instantly affect the other qubits, no matter the distance
between them.

Therefore, from a computational perspective, quantum computers are
immensely more powerful than classical computers for optimization
problems.

For instance, consider the famous Travelling Salesman Problem (TSP),
which is a classic example of an optimization problem. The TSP involves finding the shortest route between cities, such that each city
is visited only once. In the classical scenario, this problem scales fac-
torially, i.e., as $(n-1)!/2$ for n cities. Even for a modest number of

cities, this becomes computationally intense. Quantum computers, on the other hand, could potentially solve this in polynomial time, i.e., much faster than any known classical algorithm.

As Quantum Computing currently stands, a field of research named Quantum Optimization Algorithms, like Quantum Approximate Optimization Algorithm (QAOA), Variational Quantum Eigensolver (VQE), etc., focus on devising quantum algorithms to solve optimization problems more efficiently compared to classical algorithms.

Looking into the future, quantum computing could revolutionize areas like:

1. Logistics: optimisation of delivery routes, warehouse stocking etc.

2. Medicine: drug discovery, DNA sequencing etc.

3. Finance: portfolio optimization, risk analysis etc.

In conclusion, while quantum computing's full potential is yet to be realized due to the nascence of the technology, it holds immense potential in solving optimization problems much more efficiently than its classical counterpart.

8.10 Can you provide an example of an optimization problem that could benefit from a quantum approach?

Yes, one classical optimization problem that could benefit from a quantum approach is the "Traveling Salesman Problem" (TSP). The TSP is a well-known problem in the field of operations research and theoretical computer science. It asks: "Given a list of cities and the distances between each pair of cities, what is the shortest possible route that visits each city and returns to the origin city?"

As the number of cities (n) grows, the problem becomes exponentially harder to solve. This is because the number of possible solutions is

(n-1)!, i.e., the factorial of (n-1) - this number grows extremely fast
and even for modest n, it soon surpasses the computational feasibility
of classical computers.

In principle, quantum algorithms could provide significant speed-up
for solving such problems. This is because quantum computers can,
theoretically, evaluate a large number of possible solutions simultaneously, thanks to a property called superposition. This property allows
quantum bits (qubits), the basic units of quantum information, to exist in multiple states at once, unlike classical bits that can only be in
one state at a time (either 0 or 1).

One possible quantum algorithm to solve the TSP is the Quantum
Approximate Optimization Algorithm (QAOA), which has been proposed as a heuristic for finding approximate solutions to combinatorial
problems.

In terms of a specific numerical example, suppose we are tasked with
solving a TSP for 10 cities in a classical computer and in a future fault-
tolerant quantum computer capable of running the QAOA. Assuming
the cities are arranged in a grid and the distances are Euclidean, we
could have a situation like this:

Let's illustrate this situation with the following table:

Computer	Time to find solution
Classical (Exact)	Days
Classical (Heuristic)	Minutes
Quantum (Future)	Milliseconds

In this illustrative example, we can see how the quantum approach
could provide an exponential speedup for the problem.

However, it is important to mention that our current state of technology is not yet able to solve real-world instances of TSP using quantum
computers, as these systems are still in their infancy and face significant challenges, such as error correction and qubit coherence time.
But with future advances in the field of quantum computing, the
potential benefits could be enormous.

8.11 What are quantum annealers and how do they relate to optimization problems?

Quantum Annealing is one of the techniques employed in quantum computing to solve complex optimization problems. It originates from analogy to a process in material science known as annealing, whereby the material is heated and then gradually cooled to decrease its defects, leading to an optimal structural condition.

A more formal representation would be that Quantum Annealing (also called adiabatic quantum computing) is a metaheuristic for finding the global minimum of a given objective function over a given set of candidate solutions. It utilizes quantum properties such as superposition and quantum tunneling to find the minimum (or maximum) of a function.

To understand the mechanism of quantum annealers, it's essential to introduce some notions: The problem at hand is defined as H_p, the final Hamiltonian whose ground state represents the solution to the problem. The initial Hamiltonian H_i is chosen such that its ground state can be easily prepared and it doesn't commute with H_p. The time-dependent Hamiltonian is defined as $H(t) = (1 - t/T)H_i + (t/T)H_p$, where T is the total annealing time.

The Quantum Annealing (QA) process gradually evolves from the initial Hamiltonian to the problem Hamiltonian $(H_i \to H_p)$, following the minimum energy state. Ideally, it stays in the ground state of $H(t)$ throughout the evolution, if the annealing is slow enough (Adiabatic theorem).

When it comes to solving optimization problems, quantum annealing shows potential advantages. Optimization problems occur in many fields such as finance, logistics, machine learning and they often involve large calculations and combinatorial complexity. Quantum annealers try to solve these problems by taking advantage of the nature of quantum mechanics.

For instance, while classical annealing might get stuck in local minima, Quantum Annealing can escape local minima by tunneling effect, hence it's likely to find the global minimum more efficiently.

However, it should be noted that developing practical, large-scaling quantum annealers is still very challenging due to issues like decoherence and error correction. Yet, current research and development efforts in this field are vital and will ideally lead to advancements in optimization, machine learning, material science and more, in the future.

8.12   What are the challenges in using quantum computers to solve real-world optimization problems?

Quantum computing has the potential to solve complex optimization problems that are beyond the capacity of classical computers. However, using quantum computers for real-world optimization tasks is not straightforward, due to several challenges.

1. **Quantum Hardware and Scalability:** Currently, due to hardware restrictions, we don't have quantum computers with sufficient quantum bits (qubits) to solve complex real-world problems. The performance of prototype quantum devices is measured in quantum volume, which takes into account both the number of qubits and the complexity of operations that can be performed. At present, we are still in the noisy intermediate-scale quantum (NISQ) era, where quantum computers are limited and have high error rates. Scaling up quantum devices while maintaining low error rates is a significant challenge.

2. **Error Correction:** Quantum systems are very sensitive to environmental disturbances which can introduce errors in the calculations. Quantum error correction codes are used to mitigate these errors, but their implementation is quite resource-intensive and decreases the ef-

fective number of available qubits.

3. **Algorithm Development:** Developing quantum algorithms that offer a significant advantage over classical algorithms is another challenge. To leverage quantum computing's potential to solve optimization problems, you need algorithms that can effectively encode problems into a form that a quantum computer can handle.

4. **Decoherence:** Quantum information tends to rapidly decay over time, a phenomenon known as decoherence. This limits the time available for computation which, in turn, limits the complexity of the problems that can be solved.

5. **Embedding Issues:** Mapping an optimization problem onto a quantum computer (specifically, a quantum annealer such as D-Wave system) can be challenging, since it involves translating the problem into a graph where vertices denote variables and edges represent relations between these variables. If the initial problem has a structure that doesn't fit into the hardware graph, extra ancilla qubits need to be added. This makes a significant difference in the effectiveness of the optimization process.

6. **Lack of Benchmarking Standards:** Currently, we lack the widely accepted benchmarks for determining when and under what conditions quantum computers outperform classical computers on practical problems.

Here is a summary table:

It's important to note that despite these challenges, steady progress is being made and the potential of quantum computing as a powerful tool for solving complex optimization problems is undeniable.

Challenges	Description
Quantum Hardware and Scalability	Scarce numbers of qubits and difficulty on scaling up while maintaining low error rates
Error Correction	Quantum sensitivity to environmental disturbances and resource-intensive nature of error correction codes
Algorithm Development	Designing quantum-friendly algorithms that offer significant advantage over classical counterparts
Decoherence	Rapid decay of quantum information limiting computational time
Embedding Issues	Mapping or translating the problem into a quantum format
Lack of Benchmarking Standards	Absence of widely accepted standards for comparison of quantum and classical computers

8.13 How does the quantum approximate optimization algorithm (QAOA) work?

The Quantum Approximate Optimization Algorithm (QAOA) is an algorithm designed to solve combinatorial optimization problems using quantum computing. These types of problems involve finding an optimal solution (which could be the minimum or maximum) from a finite set of possible solutions.

Here's how the QAOA works:

1. **Initialization:** Start with a quantum computer in a simple state. Typically, we choose the state $|\psi\rangle = |+\rangle^{\oplus n}$, where $|+$ is a quantum superposition of $|0$ and $|1$.

2. **Applying the QAOA Circuit:** The QAOA circuit is applied
to this state. The circuit consists of two types of unitary transformations, which are applied alternately. There are p layers of these
transformations, where p is a parameter of the algorithm:

- The first type of transformation, denoted by $U(C, \gamma)$, is generated
by the classical cost function C that we wish to optimize. In this
transformation, each qubit is rotated around the Z-axis of the Bloch
sphere by an angle determined by the corresponding qubit's contri-
bution to the cost. The angles   are parameters of the QAOA that
can be adjusted to optimize the algorithm's performance.

- The second type of transformation, denoted by $U(B, \beta)$, is a standard quantum gate called a "mixer". This transformation rotates each
qubit around the X-axis of the Bloch sphere by an angle , which can
also be adjusted.

- The transformations are applied in sequence, and the final state of
the quantum computer after the QAOA circuit is denoted by $|\psi(\gamma, \beta)\rangle$.

3. **Measure and Repeat:** The state of the quantum computer
is measured, producing a bit string, which corresponds to a candidate solution of the combinatorial problem at hand. This process is
repeated many times to generate a set of bit strings.

4. **Optimize Parameters:** Evaluate the quality of the solutions
represented by the bit strings, and adjust the parameters γ, β to increase the likelihood of finding better solutions in future runs of the
algorithm. This process is often carried out with a classical optimization algorithm.

5. **Return the Best Solution:** After several iterations (often hun-
dreds or thousands), the QAOA returns the best solution it could find,
which is an approximation of the optimal solution of the problem.

In terms of applications, there's hope that QAOA could solve some
real-world problems, such as optimizing logistics, forming financial
portfolios, or predicting molecules' properties. Currently, the use
of QAOA is still very much in the research phase, but it is one of

the most promising quantum algorithms for the near-term quantum devices that we expect to see in the next 5–10 years.

Here's the corresponding QAOA circuit:

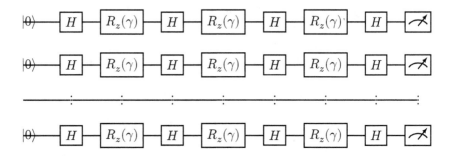

Each H represents a Hadamard gate preparing the qubit in super-position state, and Rz represents the rotation of a qubit around the Z-axis in accordance with the parameters of the problem.

Chapter 9

Challenges and Controversies in Quantum Computing

The ninth chapter confronts the challenges and controversies that pervade the quantum computing landscape. We delve into the issues of scalability, coherence time, and the debate surrounding quantum supremacy versus quantum advantage, offering a balanced perspective on the state of quantum computing.

9.1 What are the main challenges in scaling up quantum systems?

Scaling up quantum systems poses several challenges. The main ones include:

1. **Quantum Coherence**: Quantum coherence is a fundamental

principle of quantum mechanics that allows particles to be in multiple states at once, a scenario known as a superposition. This property is exploited by quantum computers to perform complex calculations. However, quantum coherence decays rapidly due to environmental interactions (a process known as decoherence) that can disrupt the quantum system. Preserving coherence long enough to run quantum algorithms is a major challenge.

2. **Error Correction**: Quantum systems are highly susceptible to errors due to the fragile nature of quantum states. Unlike classical bits, quantum bits cannot be copied due to the no-cloning theorem. This makes conventional error correction methods impossible to implement.

$$|\psi\rangle \rightarrow |\psi\rangle|\psi\rangle \quad \text{(Not Allowed)}$$

Thus, the development of quantum error correction codes like the Shor's code and Steane Code is an ongoing area of research.

3. **Physical Implementations and Cost**: Building a physical quantum computer is technologically challenging and resource-intensive. The requirements vary based on Qubits types like the Superconducting Qubits, Trapped Ion Qubits, etc. It's a challenge to achieve the tech demand at a reasonable cost.

4. **Interconnecting Qubits**: As the number of qubits increases, so does the challenge of entangling them. In a fully connected (or universal) quantum computer, any qubit can interact with any other. Achieving this scalability is a major challenge.

5. **Algorithm Development**: Despite the existence of a few optimal algorithms such as Shor's and Grover's algorithms, developing new quantum algorithms is a substantial challenge.

6. **Quantum Programming**: Quantum mechanics' unintuitive nature makes quantum programming and the development of practical quantum software a major challenge. Industry-standard software like Qiskit, Microsoft Quantum Development Kit, are easing the process,

but a lot of work remains to be done.

There's a promising ongoing work on each of these challenges, but
significant progress needs to be made before we can have scalable
quantum systems.

9.2 Why is achieving scalability critical for practical quantum computing?

Achieving scalability in quantum computing is critical because it directly influences the size and sophistication of the problems we can
solve. Unlike classical computers, where adding more transistors to
an existing chip improves its computational power, quantum computers require a delicate balancing act to increase their computational
power. This delicate balance is required because the quantum bits,
or qubits, that form the basis of quantum computing require careful
handling to maintain their delicate state of quantum superposition
and entanglement.

A quantum computer with many qubits has a computational power
that grows exponentially with the number of qubits. This principle arises from the peculiar properties of quantum mechanics. For
instance, if a quantum computer has n qubits, it can be in a superposition of up to 2^n states simultaneously. Therefore, the more qubits a
quantum computer has, the more complex the problems it can solve.

However, quantum bits are fragile. Environmental factors such as
heat and electromagnetic radiation can cause qubits to lose their
state, a phenomenon known as decoherence. Also, imperfections in
the control mechanism can lead to errors in the qubits' state, making
the computer output nonsense.

Hence, creating a quantum computer with many qubits is not enough
- these qubits must also be high-quality, i.e., they remain in a quantum state for a long time, and the errors in their control are minimal. These requirements pose a massive challenge due to technical

constraints, making it hard to build large, functional quantum computers.

Therefore, achieving scalability does not merely require increasing the number of qubits but also maintaining their quality, making it one of the most significant challenges in turning quantum computers into practical machines.

This is similar in concept to upgrading a classical computer's CPU: merely increasing the count of transistors isn't enough. The entire system, from instruction set architecture to cooling solutions, must also be optimized around the new hardware to harness its increased power effectively. But in quantum computers, this problem is magnified by the fragile nature of quantum states and the complexities of quantum mechanics.

9.3 How do different quantum computing models address scalability?

Quantum computing is at the embryonic stage of its development, with tremendous potential but also several significant challenges obstructing its adoption. One of the most prominent issues pertains to the scalability of quantum systems.

Quantum computing development falls primarily into three models: quantum gate model (also known as circuit model), adiabatic (or quantum annealing) model, and topological quantum computing. Each of these models addresses the scalability issue differently.

1. **Quantum Gate Model**

In the quantum gate model, quantum bits (qubits) are entangled and manipulated through quantum gates. To scale this model, the superimposition and entanglement of many qubits is necessary. Stable qubits are key to scalability, but noise and decoherence are significant issues practically. Error correction codes like the "surface code" can be implemented to handle these challenges efficiently. However, the tradeoff is that these error correction methods require additional qubits, which increases the system's complexity and resource requirements significantly.

The scalability can be illustrated as following:

Table 9.1: Number of Logical vs Physical Qubits

Number of Logical qubits (n)	Physical Qubits Needed (E.g. For Surface Code)
1	1000 to 10000
10	10000 to 100000
100	1,000,000 to 10,000,000

The table above shows that each logical qubit (essential for computation) in a quantum gate model may require a thousand to ten thousand physical qubits for error correction.

2. **Adiabatic Model/Quantum Annealing**

The adiabatic or quantum annealing model scales by increasing the number of quantum bits in a system. In this model, a problem is encoded into the lowest energy state of a system, and the system's current state gradually evolves to that state. It, however, involves the challenge of maintaining precision and coherence as size increases. An additional limitation is that the connectivity between qubits decreases as size increases, limiting its ability to effectively solve complex problems. Thus, designing efficient methods for encoding problems and maintaining coherence remains a major challenge for the scalability of this model.

3. **Topological Quantum Computing**

Topological quantum computing attempts to scale by leveraging anyons—quasi-particles that exist in two-dimensional systems—and their global twisted properties that make them highly resistant to local noise. They use the properties for encoding information, thus significantly reducing the number of qubits for error correction.

However, so far, we are still unable to create the types of anyons necessary for topological quantum computing, so scaling up this form of quantum computation remains a theoretical discussion.

In conclusion, all the quantum computing models have their unique ways and challenges to address the scalability, generally involving tradeoffs between error correction, connectivity, coherence time, and hardware complexity. For each model, significant theoretical and experimental work still remains to overcome these issues and achieve scalable, practical quantum computation.

9.4   How does the issue of quantum error correction relate to scalability?

Quantum error correction (QEC) and scalability are deeply intertwined in the subject of quantum computing. They form a significant part of the current challenges being faced in quantum computing advancement.

Quantum systems are highly susceptible to errors due to two primary aspects: decoherence and quantum gate imperfections. Decoherence is a process where a quantum system loses information to its environment, while imperfections in quantum gates (the building blocks of a quantum computer) may result in errors when a quantum operation is performed.

To overcome these error challenges, the concept of quantum error correction was introduced. QEC works by spreading quantum information over multiple physical qubits for protection against errors and then systematically detecting and correcting errors.

However, implementing QEC introduces a new issue of scalability. For QEC to work effectively, it requires many physical qubits to create a single logical qubit (which is protected against errors by QEC). In other words, we use redundancy in physical qubits to protect the information in a logical qubit.

For example, in the surface code error correction (one of the most
typical strategies in quantum computing), you may require approximately 1,000 physical qubits to represent a single logical qubit. So,
the more qubits you want to compute with, the larger the overhead
in physical qubits required for maintaining quantum coherence via
QEC.

Consequently, you would need an impractically high number of qubits
for any substantial computation if looking at the current state of
technology.

Here is a simple illustration of the relationship between the number of
logical qubits and the required number of physical qubits using QEC:

```
| Logical Qubits | Required Physical Qubits |
|---------------:|-------------------------:|
|              1 |                    1,000 |
|             10 |                   10,000 |
|            100 |                 1,00,000 |
```

To actually build a scalable quantum computer, improvements need
to be made on several fronts: Qubit quality (to minimise noise), QEC
techniques (to correct errors efficiently), and Qubit quantity (to have
a practical number of logical qubits). It is an active research field and
key hurdle that must be overcome to realise the potential of quantum
computing.

9.5   What potential solutions exist for achiev-
ing scalable quantum computers?

While quantum computing is very promising, several significant challenges must be overcome to develop large-scale useful quantum computers. Here are few potential solutions:

1. **Quantum Error Correction**: One of the primary issues in
quantum computing is that quantum bits (qubits) are susceptible to

noise and errors. One potential solution to such problem is the implementation of Quantum Error Correction Codes (QECCs). The extensive research in the field of QECCs has led to numerous algorithms that can detect and correct quantum errors automatically during computation, such as the Shor Code and the Steane Code.

2. **Topological Qubits**: Instead of using qubits that are prone to errors, the field of quantum computing could advance substantially with the development of more noise-resistant qubits, such as Majorana fermions or anyons that are used in topological quantum computing. The idea behind this method is to store quantum information non-locally, making it much tougher for errors to eradicate the quantum information.

3. **High Tolerance Quantum Algorithms**: These are quantum algorithms that can tolerate a higher amount of noise and errors than usual, while still producing correct outputs. An example of such a quantum algorithm in use today is the Variational Quantum Eigensolver (VQE), which doesn't require error-prone steps like quantum phase estimation.

4. **Hardware Improvements**: Lastly, many advancements in quantum hardware have led to the development of devices that are less prone to errors, have a longer coherence time, have better control over qubits, and so forth. Cutting-edge fabrication techniques and materials can improve the quality of superconducting circuits used as physical qubits, while advanced laser systems research can reduce noise and improve control precision in trapped-ion quantum systems.

5. **Quantum Software Stack Deployment**: The development of robust software and programming languages for quantum computing can streamline quantum computation and enable high-level abstractions, further enhancing the scalability and reliability of quantum systems. Frameworks such as Q# from Microsoft and QISKIT from IBM aim to make programming quantum computers more accessible, enabling better testing, debugging, and optimizing of quantum algorithms.

It's important to note that these are potential solutions, not guarantees. There's still much we don't understand about quantum information and many engineering hurdles to overcome. However, the above-mentioned solutions offer possible paths towards creating a scalable quantum computer.

9.6 What is coherence time and why is it a critical parameter in quantum computing?

Coherence time, also known as the coherence lifespan, is a critical parameter in quantum computing. In quantum physics, the coherence time is the measure of the stability of the phase relationship between the components of a wave in space and time. Formally, it is the time over which a quantum system stays in a single quantum state before transitioning into other states. The coherence time directly impacts the quality of qubits, which are the fundamental building blocks of quantum computers.

Longer coherence times are beneficial because they allow quantum information to be stored and processed over more extended periods; shorter coherence times limit the reliability and capacity of quantum computing systems to perform complex computations. Therefore, strategies to stabilize coherence time and protect fragile quantum states from noise and instability have become essential research areas in quantum computing.

In mathematical notation coherence time (T_2) is defined as:

$$T_2 = \frac{1}{\gamma}$$

where γ is the decay rate of the coherence.

Consider a single qubit which at time 't=0' is in a superposition state $\frac{1}{\sqrt{2}}(|0\rangle + |1\rangle)$. If we measure the qubit's state at different times, we observe that the probability $P_1(t)$ of the qubit being in state $|1\rangle$ decays exponentially with time as

$$P_1(t) = \frac{1}{2}\left[1 - \exp(-2t/T_2)\right],$$

where the decay rate of the function is determined by the coherence time T_2 (the time constant in the exponential decay). This implies that the coherence of the qubit state, its ability to maintain the phase relationship, decreases over time due to environmental disturbances or 'noise'.

Therefore, extending the coherence time of qubits is a fundamental challenge in developing scalable and efficient quantum computing systems. This is one of the reasons we often operate quantum computers at ultra-cold temperatures, to minimize environmental disturbances, and invest significantly in developing error correction protocols.

Let me know if you need more details or if you want to discuss further other challenges and controversies in quantum computing.

9.7 How do quantum engineers work to increase coherence times in quantum systems?

Coherence time is a significant measure in quantum computing as it represents the time frame over which a quantum system can retain its quantum properties. Maintaining and increasing this coherence time poses a big challenge for quantum engineers. Here are a few methods that quantum engineers adopt.

1. **Materials Choices and System Design Changes:** Quantum en-

gineers experiment with different types of materials and design alter-
ations to enhance the lifespan of quantum bits. For instance, engineers opt for superconducting circuits or topological qubits that have
longer coherence times.

For instance, the Josephson junction-based superconducting qubits
have evolved significantly over time to reduce noise and enhance coherence. These qubits are often isolated as much as possible from the
environment to avoid decoherence caused by environmental factors.

2. **Error Correction Mechanisms:** To rectify coherence loss, quantum error correction codes (QECs) are employed. QEC codes aid in
detecting and correcting errors without causing measurement (which
would lead to decoherence).

One example is the Shor code which encodes a single qubit into 9
qubits, thereby improving the chances of correcting any errors that
occur due to decoherence.

3. **Dynamical Decoupling:** Dynamical decoupling (DD) is another technique used to fight coherence loss. This is a sequence of
control operations applied on quantum bits such that the overall interaction with the environment is minimized.

These operations are specially designed such that they do not affect
the quantum information stored in the qubits, but only aim to de-
couple the qubits from the surrounding noise sources.

4. **Cooling down of Quantum Systems:** Since quantum systems
are highly sensitive to thermal fluctuations, they are required to be
operated at extremely low temperatures. This minimises the environmental interference hence increasing the coherence times.

Techniques used to cool down quantum systems include dilution re-
frigerators that can reach temperatures close to absolute zero (millikelvin range).

5. **Use of Low-Noise Electronics:** Another commonly used method
is the implementation of low-noise electronics. High quality electron-

ics produce less heat and, in turn, less noise, which is crucial for coherence.

An overview of strategies to increase coherence times:

Table 9.2: Mitigation Methods

Method	Description
Materials Choices	Superconducting or topological qubits
Error Correction Mechanisms	Quantum Error Correction codes like Shor code
Dynamical Decoupling	Sequence of operations to minimize interaction with environment
System Cooling	Lowering temperatures to minimize thermal fluctuations
Low-Noise Electronics	Electronics that produce less heat and noise

In truth, coherence time improvement is multi-factorial engineering problem and typically requires optimization of all of these factors to achieve significantly longer coherence times.

9.8 How does coherence time limit the complexity of quantum computations that can be performed?

Coherence time refers to the amount of time a quantum system can remain in a coherent state, i.e., where quantum computation can be performed effectively. It's essentially how long a quantum bit or "qubit" can maintain its quantum state before being disturbed by its environment causing what we call decoherence.

In a quantum computer, calculations are performed by applying a
sequence of quantum gates (operations) to qubits. Each quantum gate
takes a certain amount of time to perform, so the more quantum gates
a computation requires, the longer it will take to execute. However,
the computation needs to be completed within the coherence time;
if this doesn't happen, the qubits lose their quantum state, and the
computation cannot be reliably completed.

Hence, the coherence time directly limits the number of quantum
gates, and thereby the complexity of quantum computations that
can be performed. A longer coherence time would allow more computations to be performed.

If T_{op} is the operating time for a single gate and T_{coh} is the coherence time, the number of operations (N) that can be performed is
approximately $N = \frac{T_{coh}}{T_{op}}$.

For example, if a single operation takes 10 ns (nanoseconds) and
the coherence time is 100 s (microseconds), approximately 10,000
operations can be performed before decoherence.

The need for high coherence times is even more critical considering
error correction principles in quantum computing, which require multiple physical qubits to encode and correct errors in a logical qubit.
Additionally, increasing the number of qubits while maintaining the
same average coherence time is a challenge.

Improving the coherence times of qubits is a major research challenge
in the field of quantum computing to enable the execution of complex
quantum algorithms.

Tackling this challenge will require new materials, chip designs, and
error correction techniques. Nonetheless, the coherence time has seen
improvements over recent years due to advances in engineering techniques and theoretical understanding.

9.9 What strategies are being explored to overcome limitations imposed by short coherence times?

Coherence time, or T_2 time, is a crucial parameter in quantum computing which dictates the lifetime of a quantum state. Imposed by environmental noise and imperfections in quantum devices, the short coherence times present physical challenges to sustaining quantum information storage, manipulation, and readout.

Given this challenge, many strategies have been explored to increase coherence time and improve the robustness of quantum computing. Here are some of them:

1. **Hardware Improvements**: By improving the physical setup and the materials used in quantum systems, the environmental noise can be reduced. This includes using high quality materials, better shielding, and advanced fabrication processes. For example, in the case of superconducting qubits, breakthroughs in alloying and surface treatments have led to significant improvements in T_2 times.

2. **Dynamical Decoupling**: This is a method of 'refocusing' a quantum state by applying a series of rapid control pulses. This serves the purpose of negating the effects of slow environmental noise and thus preserving the quantum state. In essence, this method tries to 'average out' the noise effects over time.

3. **Quantum Error Correction (QEC)**: QEC is a method of detecting and correcting errors in quantum bits (qubits) without directly measuring them, thus preserving their quantum state. It involves encoding logical qubits using multiple physical qubits and leveraging the fact that most errors in quantum systems are local to effectively suppress them.

4. **Topological Quantum Computing**: This approach rests on the use of anyons, particles that are neither bosons nor fermions and exist only in two dimensions. As a result of their unique properties,

manipulations of anyons are topologically protected and extremely
resistant to decoherence. Although this approach requires significant
technological breakthroughs and is still mostly theoretical, it is one
of the most promising long-term strategies to overcome the short T_2
times.

5. **Computational Techniques**: Techniques such as Quantum
Annealing or the Variational Quantum Eigensolver (VQE) are designed to leverage the advantages of quantum systems while mitigat-
ing the impact of short coherence times. They are hybrid quantum-
classical algorithms that involve minimal quantum coherence time,
which means that the effect of short coherence time can be lessened.

Here, it's important to note that these strategies have trade-offs
in terms of complexity, practicality, and scalability. While long-
term strategies may offer comprehensive solutions, they often require
substantial advances in technology and understanding. In contrast,
short-term strategies may be more implementable but might not fully
address the challenges posed by quantum decoherence. This suggests
that a hybrid or multi-faceted approach might be beneficial in over-
coming limitations imposed by short coherence times.

9.10 How does coherence time relate to the fault-tolerance of a quantum computer?

Coherence time is a critical factor in the fault-tolerance and overall
functionality of a quantum computer. It refers to the time duration
for which a quantum system retains its quantum state before transitioning to a classical system due to environmental factors (often
referred to as 'decoherence').

A relatively shorter coherence time may limit the time available to run
quantum computations and correct errors, resulting in more potential
faults. On the other hand, a longer coherence time creates more

extended intervals in which quantum operations can be performed and errors can be corrected, making the system more fault-tolerant.

The error threshold theorem is the key concept behind fault-tolerant quantum computing. The theorem asserts that given the physical error rate of quantum operations is below a certain threshold, it is possible to perform a practically-long quantum computation with an arbitrarily low logical error rate- provided sufficient error-correction overhead.

Coherence time directly impacts the physical error rate. Therefore, we can say that the longer the coherence time, the better chance we have of the physical error rate being beneath the threshold, and thus, the better chance the quantum system has of being fault-tolerant.

So, when we talk about fault-tolerance in quantum computing, we're essentially talking about the management of quantum error rates, which are directly influenced by coherence time, gate operation time, and the specifics of the implementation technology.

Coherence Time	Error Rate	Fault Tolerance
Long	Low	High
Short	High	Low

In essence, meeting quantum computing's fault-tolerance needs is a balancing act involving coherence time and other factors. While a longer coherence time is desired for more fault tolerance, practical limits on how long qubits can maintain their state should be considered. This all needs to be taken into account when attempting to build a functional, scalable, and usable quantum computer.

Further research is required to improve the coherence times while making the gate operations faster without increasing the physical error, all at the same time. As the field of quantum computing grows, such issues will continue to present essential areas for research and study.

Chapter 10

Resources and Quantum Programming

In our final chapter, we transition from theory to practice, introducing quantum programming languages and discussing popular quantum computing platforms like IBM Q and Google Quantum AI. This chapter equips you with practical knowledge and resources to embark on your own quantum coding journey.

10.1 What are the main quantum programming languages as of now?

Quantum computing has witnessed rapid advancements in recent years, leading to the development and evolution of several quantum programming languages. Some of the most notable ones include:

1. **Q# (Microsoft Quantum Development Kit)**: Q# is a high-level quantum-focused language developed by Microsoft. It is fully

integrated into the .NET platform and comes with quantum-specific data types and operations. It offers a hybrid model which allows for the combination of quantum and classical components in a program.

2. **Qiskit (IBM)**: Qiskit is an open-source quantum computing platform that enables developers to build quantum applications. Developers can use Python-based Qiskit to create and run quantum computing programs on quantum computers over the cloud.

3. **Forest (Rigetti Computing)**: Forest is a quantum programming platform from Rigetti Computing. Its primary language is Quil (Quantum Instruction Language). It profits from a Python-based high-level programming environment.

4. **Cirq (Google)**: Google's Cirq is a Python library for writing, manipulating, and optimizing quantum circuits and running them against quantum computers and simulators.

5. **Strawberry Fields (Xanadu)**: Strawberry Fields is a full-stack Python library for designing, optimizing, and simulating photonic quantum circuits.

6. **Silq (ETH Zurich)**: Silq is a high-level quantum programming language that focuses on safe automatic uncomputation, making it less prone to quantum bugs.

Here's a basic comparison table:

These are just few of the many languages being developed to write quantum algorithms and programs. A developer's choice would depend on the quantum technology (superconducting, ion trap, topological, photonic etc.) being used, as well as the specific requirements of the algorithm or application being developed.

Table 10.1: Quantum Programming Languages

Programming Language	Provider	Language Type	Linked Technology
Q#	Microsoft	High-level, .NET integrated	Microsoft Quantum Development Kit
Qiskit	IBM	Python-based	IBM Quantum systems
Forest, Quil	Rigetti	Python-based	Rigetti Quantum systems
Cirq	Google	Python-based	Google Quantum Computing Service
Strawberry Fields	Xanadu	Python-based	Xanadu Quantum systems
Silq	ETH Zurich	High-level	Independent, academic

10.2 How do quantum programming languages differ from classical ones?

Quantum programming languages significantly differ from classical ones, mainly owing to the fundamental differences between classical and quantum computing itself. Classical programming revolves around bits that exist in two states, 0 or 1, whereas quantum programming incorporates quantum bits (qubits) that can exist in a state of superposition—being both 0 and 1 simultaneously—which allows exponentially more complex computing processes.

Below are specific ways in which quantum programming languages differ from classical ones:

1. **Superposition.** In the quantum computing model, a quantum

bit (qubit) can exist not just in the state of 0 or 1 like traditional bits in classical computers, but also in states where they can be both 0 and 1 at the exact same time. Thus, computations on qubits can be done for a range of possible numbers simultaneously. A quantum programming language must be able to handle and operate on these superpositions, unlike classical programming languages that only operate on individual bits.

An example in Q# (Microsoft's quantum programming language), we express a superimposed state with a Hadamard gate:

```
using (q = Qubit()) // Allocate a qubit.
{
    H(q); // Put the qubit to superposition state.
}
```

2. **Entanglement.** Quantum programming languages allow for the entanglement of qubits. This is a unique property of quantum systems where qubits become interrelated, allowing the state of one qubit to directly influence the others, regardless of the distance between them. Classical programming languages do not have an equivalent concept.

For instance, with Q#, we can create an entangled pair using a Controlled Pauli-Z operation ('CNOT'):

```
using (qs = Qubit[2]) // Allocate 2 qubits.
{
    H(qs[0]); // Put the first qubit in a superposition state.
    CNOT(qs[0], qs[1]); // Entangle the first and the second qubit.
}
```

3. **Unitarity.** All transformations of qubits in quantum computing systems are unitary. Unitary operations are reversible, meaning that no information is lost during the computation. In comparison, classical programming languages are generally not designed with reversibility in mind.

For example, a unitary gate in Q# could be the Pauli-X gate ('X'), which flips the state of a qubit:

```
using (q = Qubit()) // Allocate a qubit.
{
    X(q); // Flip the state of the qubit.
}
```

```
}
```

4. **Measurements.** In quantum computing, measurements change the state of the system, collapsing superpositions into classical states (0 or 1). In contrast, observing or reading the state of a classical system does not alter the system.

Like this measurement operation presented in Q#:

```
using (q = Qubit()) // Allocate a qubit.
{
    H(q); // Put the qubit in a superposition state.
    let res = M(q); // Measure the state of the qubit.
}
```

Quantum programming languages incorporate the peculiarities of quantum mechanics within their constructs, enabling developers to manipulate and reason about quantum states and phenomena. Despite these differences, quantum programming languages also draw on many concepts from classical programming, such as modularity and control flow, making them fairly accessible to classically trained programmers.

10.3 What features should a quantum programming language ideally have?

A good quantum programming language should ideally have the following features:

1. **High-Level Abstraction**: The language should be able to insulate the programmer from the underlying physics while still allowing control over quantum states, operations, and measurements. This includes support for mathematic operators that let developers manipulate quantum data.

2. **Circuit Model Representation**: It should support the circuit model of quantum computation, that is, quantum bits (qubits), quan-

tum gates, quantum circuits, quantum teleportation and the like.

3. **Quantum Data Structures**: The language should be able to represent quantum registers, quantum states, superposition, entanglement, and quantum operators. Also, it should support data structures to hold the result of quantum operations.

4. **Hybrid Programming**: Since pure quantum computers are not yet a reality, the language should be able to integrate well with classical languages to support hybrid computation tasks, which interleave classical and quantum computations.

5. **Error Correction**: Support for quantum error correction techniques is a crucial feature. Quantum computers are highly prone to errors. Ideally, the language should offer built-in support for handling these errors.

6. **Optimization Mechanisms**: The language should feature quantum-specific optimization, to reduce the quantum cost of computations.

7. **Simulator and Real Hardware Compatibility**: The quantum language must be compatible with both quantum simulators and quantum hardware for testing and debugging purposes.

8. **Extendability**: It should allow adding quantum libraries for certain specific applications, such as quantum cryptography, teleportation etc.

9. **Well-defined syntax and Semantics**: Like any other programming language, a quantum language also needs to have a well-defined syntax and semantics so that it is easy to use and understand for programmers.

10. **Usability and Learnability**: Despite being rooted in complex physics, the language should be accessible enough for software developers and researchers who do not have an extensive background in quantum mechanics.

Here is a simple example of Quantum Teleportation in Q# Quatum

Programming language:

```
operation TeleportClassicalMessageTest () : Unit {
    let message = [true, false];
    using (register = Qubit[3]) {
        ApplyToEach(H, register);
        TeleportClassicalMessage(register[0], register[1], message[0]);
        TeleportClassicalMessage(register[1], register[2], message[1]);
        let data = [MResetZ(register[0]), MResetZ(register[1]), MResetZ(
            register[2])];
        mutable i = 0;
        ApplyToEach(MResetZ, register);
        for (received in data) {
            Fact(received == message[i], $"Received␣{received},␣expected␣{
                message[i]}");
            set i += 1;
        }
    }
}
```

Note that the code applies a Hadamard gate to each qubit in a register, and then it uses the operation 'TeleportClassicalMessage' to teleport the classical message. At the end, the Fact function asserts that the teleported message is the same as the sent one.

10.4   How can one design and implement a quantum algorithm using a quantum programming language?

Designing and implementing a quantum algorithm requires a grasp of quantum computing concepts like qubits, quantum gates, and superposition, as well as knowledge of a quantum programming language like Q# from Microsoft, Qiskit from IBM, or Google's Cirq. Here's a general overview of the steps you would typically take:

1. **Understand the Problem:** Quantum algorithms are more efficient than their classical counterparts for only a handful of specific problems. This step involves understanding the problem domain and determining if a quantum algorithm would offer an advantage.

2. **Design the Algorithm:** This is the theoretical stage where you

come up with the quantum algorithm. This would involve designing a quantum circuit that solves the problem using the principles of quantum mechanics. You'll need to conceptualize the relevant qubits, quantum gates, any required quantum teleportation, etc. The design would be an abstract representation often conveyed through a circuit diagram.

3. **Choose the Quantum Language:** Next, choose the most suitable quantum programming language based on the requirements of your project. Common languages include Q#, Qiskit, and Cirq, and each has its own unique features and advantages. For example, Q# integrates with .NET and works well for quantum algorithm prototyping, while Qiskit allows for both high-level and low-level interface design.

4. **Implement the Algorithm:** Translate the algorithm design into code using your chosen quantum programming language. This generally involves preparing the qubits, applying quantum gates, and measuring the qubits.

5. **Test and Debug:** After coding the algorithm, run it on a simulator to verify its correctness. If the results aren't expected, debug and tweak the algorithm as necessary.

6. **Run the Algorithm:** Run the algorithm on a real quantum computer, if possible. IBM offers cloud access to quantum computers via IBM Q Experience. This allows developers to test their quantum algorithms on real quantum hardware.

Here's an example of a simple quantum algorithm implementation using Qiskit. This implements a quantum circuit that puts a single qubit in a superposition state:

```
import qiskit as q
QC = q.QuantumCircuit(1) # Create a quantum circuit with one qubit
QC.h(0)                  # Apply a Hadamard gate to put the qubit in
     superposition
QC.measure_all()         # Measure the qubit
QC.draw()                # Draw the quantum circuit
```

In this snippet, 'QC = q.QuantumCircuit(1)' creates a qubit. 'QC.h(0)' applies a Hadamard gate to put the qubit in a superposition. 'QC.measure_all()' measures the qubit, collapsing the superposition to either 0 or 1. Finally, 'QC.draw()' outputs a visual representation of the quantum circuit.

This is a basic example, but building more complex quantum algorithms would follow a similar process. Additional gates, entanglement and other quantum features could be incorporated depending on the problem and the design of the quantum algorithm.

10.5 How does one simulate a quantum algorithm using a quantum programming language?

Simulating a quantum algorithm involves creating a representation of a quantum state and the operation performed on these methods. The vectorized nature of quantum states and operator math, as well as operations like tensor products, lends themselves to the array-based processing capabilities of languages such as Python, MATLAB, etc.

As an example, let's consider a simple quantum circuit composed of two qubits with a Hadamard gate applied to the first qubit and a Controlled-Not (CNOT) gate applied to both.

Using the python quantum programming library "Qiskit", let's first install it:

```
pip install qiskit
```

Then write our simple simulation:

```
from qiskit import QuantumCircuit, execute, Aer

# Create a Quantum Circuit acting on two qubits
circ = QuantumCircuit(2)

# Add a H gate on qubit 0
circ.h(0)
```

```
# Add a CX (CNOT) gate on control qubit 0 and target qubit 1
circ.cx(0, 1)

# Visualise the circuit
print(circ)

# Choose a quantum simulator from Aer
simulator = Aer.get_backend('qasm_simulator')

# Execute the circuit on the qasm simulator
job = execute(circ, simulator)

# Grab the results from the job
result = job.result()

# Returns counts
counts = result.get_counts(circ)
print("nTotal␣counts␣are:",counts)
```

After running this code, the program creates a quantum circuit, performs operations on it, executes those operations with a simulated backend, and returns the counts of the quantum states of the final system (after measurement mentioned implicitly in 'result.get_counts()').

At this stage, it's essential to note that simulating large quantum systems can become computationally demanding due to the increase in system size, growing exponentially, a predicament known as "quantum supremacy".

Beyond basic simulation, there are more intricate details to quantum programming such as quantum error correction, compilation to specific hardware topologies, programming paradigms (procedural vs. functional), and quantum network protocols, which require additional training and literacy in quantum mechanics and quantum information science.

Also, a variety of programming languages and frameworks are available for quantum programming, from Python libraries (Qiskit, Cirq, Pennylane) to specialized languages (Q#, Silq), each with its advantages, disadvantages and particular design philosophies, as well as hardware constraints.

10.6   What are the main platforms available for quantum computing today?

There are several platforms for quantum computing available today. Here are the leading ones:

1. **IBM Quantum Experience (Qiskit)**: IBM Quantum Experience is a cloud-based platform that allows users to run algorithms and experiments, work with quantum circuits, and explore tutorials and simulations around quantum computing. Qiskit is the open-source software development kit (SDK) provided by IBM to work with their quantum processor.

With the SDK, you can create and manipulate quantum circuits and execute them on a real quantum computer. You can also use it to run quantum programs on their quantum processors for free through their cloud service.

2. **Google Quantum Computing Service (Cirq)**: Google's cloud-based quantum computing service uses Cirq, an open-source Python library for writing, manipulating, and optimizing quantum circuits and running them against quantum computers and simulators.

3. **Microsoft Quantum Development Kit (Q#)**: Microsoft's Quantum Development Kit is another excellent tool for quantum programming. It includes Q#, a high-level quantum-focused programming language, and allows for integration with Visual Studio and VS Code environments.

4. **Amazon Braket**: Amazon Braket is a fully managed service that allows scientists, researchers, and developers to start experimenting with quantum computers from different hardware providers (like D-Wave, IonQ, and Rigetti) in a single place.

5. **D-Wave Leap**: The D-Wave Leap is a cloud-based platform for quantum computing that is particularly focused on 'quantum annealing'. It allows researchers to submit their problems and uses quantum

annealing to find solutions.

6. **Alibaba Cloud Quantum Development Platform (Aliquantum)**: Alibaba's quantum development platform offers a wide range of quantum software and hardware resources and is aligned with their cloud computing services.

7. **Strawberry Fields and PennyLane by Xanadu**: Xanadu offers both photonic quantum computing hardware and software. Strawberry Fields is a Python library for simulating and executing programs on photonic quantum hardware. PennyLane is a Python library for differentiable programming of quantum computers, combining quantum with machine learning.

Each of these platforms has different capabilities and hardware systems, such as superconducting qubits, trapped ions, or photonic qubits. Moreover, each has its scripting language. Some of these platforms allow you to execute tasks on a quantum processor via a cloud interface, while others are more geared towards simulations of quantum algorithms.

10.7   How do these platforms differ in terms of capabilities and ease of use?

There are a number of platforms available for quantum programming, each with its own unique set of features and tools. Below, I compare some of the most widely used platforms:

1. IBM's Qiskit

Capabilities: Qiskit includes tools for creating and manipulating quantum programs and running them on prototype quantum devices and simulators. It also provides tools for quantum chemistry, optimization, machine learning, and quantum education.

Ease of Use: Qiskit provides comprehensive, user-friendly documentation and offers a Python-based, high-level programming interface. It is ideal for those who are familiar with Python.

2. Rigetti's Forest

Capabilities: Forest includes tools for writing quantum programs and running them on Rigetti's quantum processors or high-performance quantum simulators. It also includes Quil–the Quantum Instruction Language, QVM – the Quantum Virtual Machine, and Grove – the quantum algorithms library.

Ease of Use: Forest also uses a Python-based interface and is relatively easy to use, particularly for those with a background in Python.

3. Google's Cirq

Capabilities: Cirq is a Python library for writing, manipulating, and optimizing quantum circuits and then running them on quantum computers and simulators. It is primarily focused on near-term experiments.

Ease of Use: Like IBM's Qiskit and Rigetti's Forest, Cirq also uses a Python-based programming interface. However, it is relatively new and perhaps a bit less mature in its offerings compared to Qiskit and Forest.

4. D-Wave's Ocean SDK

Capabilities: Ocean SDK is a suite of tools provided by D-Wave systems for solving hard problems using quantum annealing. It includes tools for building quantum models and running them on D-Wave's quantum annealers.

Ease of Use: It is relatively simple to use, especially for those specifically interested in quantum annealing.

5. Microsoft's Q#

Capabilities: Q# is a domain-specific language used for expressing quantum algorithms along with the high-level classical language features needed to create practical applications. It comes with Quantum Development Kit that contains rich libraries and Quantum Simulators.

Ease of Use: It has integrated development environment setup in Visual Studio and has extensive libraries about quantum computing but it has slightly higher learning curve if users aren't familiar with C#-like languages.

Generally, the choice of platform depends on the specific needs and familiarity with the languages.

The table below summarizes these features:

Platform	Capabilities	Ease of Use
IBM's Qiskit	Quantum program creation, manipulation and running	Python-based, user-friendly
Rigetti's Forest	Quantum program creation, manipulating and running	Python-based, user-friendly
Google's Cirq	Quantum circuit manipulation, optimization and running	Python-based, newer and less mature
D-Wave's Ocean SDK	Quantum annealing, model creation, problem solving	Relatively simple to use for those interested in quantum annealing
Microsoft's Q#	High-level quantum algorithms and application creation	IDE setup in Visual Studio, C#-like language familiarity required.

Table 10.2: Comparison of different Quantum Computing Platforms

10.8   How can one start running quantum programs on these platforms?

Starting to run quantum programs involves understanding quantum concepts and the principles of quantum computing, gaining knowledge about Qubits and quantum gates, learning quantum programming languages, and utilizing cloud-based quantum computing platforms. Here several steps to start running quantum programs:

1. **Learn Quantum computing concepts:** Start by learning about Quantum Mechanics, Quantum Information Theory, Qubits, Superposition, Entanglement, and Quantum gates. Many free resources are available online such as Quantum Computing for the Very Curious. Another excellent book to start with would be "Quantum Computation and Quantum Information" by Michael Nielsen and Isaac Chuang.

2. **Learn Quantum programming languages:** A few quantum programming languages exist, and picking the right one depends on the specific research or application. Some most important quantum languages are Qiskit by IBM, Q# by Microsoft, and Cirq by Google.

* Qiskit is used with IBM's Q Experience devices and is based on Python. A great resource for learning Qiskit is the Qiskit Textbook.

* Q# is Microsoft's quantum language, integrated with their .NET platform. Microsoft also has comprehensive learning resources for Q#.

* Google's Cirq is another quantum language focusing on NISQ (Noisy Intermediate-Scale Quantum) computers.

3. **Access Quantum Computing Services:** There are several cloud-based platforms where quantum programs can be run, such as IBM Quantum Experience, Microsoft Quantum Development Kit, Google Quantum Computing Service, and Rigetti Quantum Computing Services.

4. **Run your Quantum program:** Once you're set with the theoretical concepts, programming language, and access to a quantum
computer, you can start writing and running quantum programs (also
known as quantum circuits). These programs essentially involve creating a set number of qubits, applying quantum gates, and measuring
the qubits. An example of a quantum circuit in Qiskit is:

```
from qiskit import QuantumCircuit

# Create a Quantum Circuit acting on a quantum register of three qubits
circ = QuantumCircuit(3)

# Add a H gate on qubit 0
circ.h(0)

# Add a CX (CNOT) gate on control qubit 0, and target qubit 1
circ.cx(0, 1)

# Add a CX (CNOT) gate on control qubit 0, and target qubit 2
circ.cx(0, 2)

print(circ)
```

This code will print out:

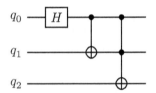

This is an example of a simple quantum circuit that creates an entangled state between 3 qubits frequently referred to as a GHZ state.

Remember, while the steps are straightforward, quantum programming involves a steep learning curve and challenges the traditional
perspectives of computation. But with continuous learning and practice, you can master the art of quantum programming.

Completing online courses, participating in quantum coding challenges, and contributing to open-source quantum computing projects
can further enhance your skills in running quantum programs.

10.9   What resources are available for learning to use these platforms effectively?

There are several resources available for learning quantum computing and quantum programming. These resources range from textbooks and online courses to software development kits (SDKs) and quantum computing simulators. Here's a short list of several useful resources:

1. **Textbooks & Academic Papers**

- "Quantum Computation and Quantum Information" by Michael A. Nielsen and Isaac L. Chuang. Arguably the most well known and respected textbook on the topic.

- "Quantum Computing: An Applied Approach" by Jack D. Hidary provides a practical approach to quantum computing focusing on coding.

- "Quantum Computing for Computer Scientists" by Noson S. Yanofsky and Mirco A. Mannucci offers a introductory quantum computing concepts focusing on mathematics and computer science.

2. **Online Courses**

- "Quantum Information Science" by MITx on the edX platform.

- "Introduction to Quantum Computing" by Saint Petersburg State University on Coursera.

- "Quantum Computing for the Determined" by Michael Nielsen on YouTube provides a clear introduction to the topic without assuming a background in physics.

3. **Quantum Programming SDKs**

- Qiskit, developed by IBM, is an open-source SDK in Python for developing quantum computing programs and running them on actual quantum computers or simulators.

- D-Wave provides Ocean SDK for developing programming skills for its quantum annealing hardware.

- Microsoft's Quantum Development Kit includes the Q# language for writing quantum algorithms.

4. **Quantum Computer Simulators**

- Quantum Inspire by QuTech is a web-based platform that allows you to build and run quantum algorithms.

- Quirk is a drag-and-drop quantum circuit simulator that runs in your browser.

5. **Documentations & Tutorials**

- IBM Qiskit has a rich set of documentation, tutorials, and sample code.

- Rigetti provides Forest SDK documentation, tutorials, and guides to help get started with its quantum computing technologies.

- Microsoft also offers extensive documentation on its Quantum Development Kit and Q# language.

6. **Blogs & Community Forums**

- Quantum Computing Stack Exchange is an active forum to ask questions and discuss topics in quantum computation.

- Quantum.country, a website developed by Michael Nielsen, offers a unique reading experience that is engaging and well-suited to the subject matter.

Remember that quantum computing is a fairly new and rapidly-growing field, so the quality and quantity of resources are ever-increasing. Don't be afraid to dive in and start teaching yourself about this exciting new branch of technology!

10.10 What is the importance of having access to real quantum hardware through these platforms?

Access to real quantum hardware through dedicated quantum programming platforms is crucial for a multitude of reasons related to both practical application and fundamental research.

1. **Development and Testing of Quantum Algorithms**: Quantum algorithms are significantly different from conventional ones in terms of both development and implementation. Direct access to quantum hardware allows the creation and testing of these algorithms in an environment they are built for.

2. **Learning and Research**: Direct interaction with quantum hardware can provide invaluable learning opportunities for both students and researchers. It allows for testing theoretical knowledge in practice, developing crucial understanding and insight into the practical behavior of quantum systems and algorithms.

3. **Capability Expansion:** Real hardware access makes it possible to constantly expand quantum capabilities as the technology develops. It allows researchers to push the limits of quantum computing and explore areas that were previously thought to be inaccessible.

4. **Advancing Quantum Technology**: Direct access to real quantum hardware can hasten the invention and improvement of quantum technologies. Current quantum computing systems are noisy and error-prone. To improve them and make them more practical, active research into quantum error correction, noise reduction, and gate fidelity improvement is necessary, which requires direct access to quantum hardware.

5. **Benchmarking and Verification**: Quantum hardware gives a ground truth for researchers and developers to benchmark and validate quantum simulators, algorithms, protocols, and other abstractions.

Due to the immature state of quantum technologies, cloud-based services like IBM's Quantum Experience, Google's Quantum Computing Service, and Rigetti's Quantum Cloud Services are providing essential platforms for researchers, developers, and businesses to engage with real quantum devices. As these technologies continue to mature and become more accessible, the importance of real hardware access and these service platforms will continue to grow.

AFTERWORD

As we traverse the final lines of this odyssey into quantum computing, I trust that the journey has been both enlightening and captivating. We have ventured into the enigmatic realm of qubits and superposition, tangled with entanglement, and decrypted the complex algorithms of quantum computation.

"Quantum Computing: Questions and Answers" was conceived as a conduit to the realm of quantum, designed to bridge the chasm between the intimidatingly abstract and the graspable. It is my fervent hope that the questions and answers within these pages have guided you in such a way, illuminating the foggy path and teasing out the sheer wonder that quantum computing inspires.

It is important, though, to acknowledge that this book is not the end of your journey. Rather, it serves as an auspicious point of departure—a beacon guiding you towards further exploration and understanding. Quantum computing is a rapidly evolving discipline, the frontiers of which are continuously expanding. This dynamic, relentless progression is what makes the field not only challenging but also irresistibly enticing.

The practicalities and challenges of quantum computing have been given equal billing in our discourse. It is hoped that this balanced perspective instills not just an understanding of quantum computation but also an appreciation of the real-world constraints and hurdles that exist. The perfect fusion of theory and practice is, after all, what steers innovation and discovery.

This book aimed to cater to the needs of diverse readers. If you were a novice when you first opened these pages, I trust that you now find yourself on a solid footing, your interest in quantum computing piqued. For the seasoned scholar, I hope that this journey has brought fresh insights and perspectives or perhaps sparked new questions in your mind.

Above all else, it is the spirit of curiosity and inquiry that has led us through this explorative journey, and it is this spirit that will propel you further into the mesmerizing domain of quantum. I encourage you to continue questioning, continue exploring, and continue discovering, for it is within these endeavors that true understanding is nurtured.

In the realm of quantum computing, the only certainty is the exciting uncertainty that lies ahead. Let's continue to embrace it, relishing the thrill of learning, the joy of discovery, and the awe-inspiring realization that we are at the forefront of defining the future of computation.

Here's to our shared journey into the quantum world. I look forward to witnessing the milestones you will undoubtedly achieve as we venture further into this exhilarating realm—one quantum bit at a time.

Carry forth the quantum curiosity. Until we meet again on the quantum path, farewell and godspeed.